Copyright © 2023 by Maxwell J. Aromano (Author)
All rights reserved. No part of this book may be reproduced or utilized in any form or by any means, electronic or mechanical, including photocopying, recording or by any information storage and retrieval system, without permission in writing from the publisher, except for brief quotations in critical articles or reviews.

The content of this book is based on various sources and is intended for educational and entertainment purposes only. While the author has made every effort to ensure the accuracy, completeness, and reliability of the information provided, the information may be subject to errors, omissions, or inaccuracies. Therefore, the author makes no warranties, express or implied, regarding the content of this book.

Readers are advised to seek the guidance of a licensed professional before attempting any techniques or actions outlined in this book. The author is not responsible for any losses, damages, or injuries that may arise from the use of information contained within. The information provided in this book is not intended to be a substitute for professional advice, and readers should not rely solely on the information presented.

By reading this book, readers acknowledge that the author is not providing legal, financial, medical, or professional advice. Any reliance on the information contained in this book is solely at the reader's own risk.

Thank you for selecting this book as a valuable source of knowledge and inspiration. Our aim is to provide you with insights and information that will enrich your understanding and enhance your personal growth. We appreciate your decision to embark on this journey of discovery with us, and we hope that this book will exceed your expectations and leave a lasting impact on your life.

Title: Crafting a Beer Renaissance: From Micro to Macrobrews
Subtitle: Exploring the Artistry and Diversity of Modern Craft Beer

Series: Ale Ages: Tracing the Timeline of Beer
Author: Maxwell J. Aromano

Table of Contents

Introduction 5
The Resurgence of Craft Beer 5
The Scope of This Book 9
The Impact of Craft Beer on the Brewing Landscape 13

Chapter 1: The Birth of Microbreweries 16
The Early Days of Microbrewing 16
The Founding Fathers of Craft Beer 20
Microbrewing Techniques and Innovation 24
The Impact of Microbreweries on Local Economies 28

Chapter 2: Exploring Craft Beer Styles 32
The Diversity of Craft Beer 32
Ales, Lagers, and Beyond 36
Hybrid Styles and Creative Brewing 41
Regional Craft Beer Specialties 45

Chapter 3: The Brewpub Revolution 49
The Emergence of Brewpubs 49
The Role of Brewpubs in the Craft Beer Movement 52
The Experience of Brewing and Dining Together 57
Successful Brewpub Models 61

Chapter 4: Independent Craft Brewers and the Fight for Authenticity 65
Defining Craft Beer and Independence 65
Craft Brewers Association and the Independent Seal 69
The Challenges of Staying Independent 73
Authenticity in Craft Brewing 77

Chapter 5: The Craft Beer Boom and Its Impact on the Beer Industry 81
The Growth of the Craft Beer Segment 81
Craft Beer's Influence on Consumer Preferences 85
Big Beer's Response to the Craft Beer Boom 89
The Impact on Global Beer Trends 94

Chapter 6: The Art and Science of Craft Brewing .. 99
Mastering the Craft of Brewing 99
The Role of Ingredients in Craft Beer 104
The Creative Process of Craft Beer Development 109
Brewing Innovation and Experimentation 114

Chapter 7: Craft Beer Culture and Community 118
The Rise of Beer Enthusiasts and Connoisseurs 118
Beer Festivals and Events 123
The Role of Online Communities 128
The Social Aspect of Craft Beer 133

Conclusion 137
Celebrating the Craft Beer Renaissance 137
The Ongoing Evolution of the Craft Beer Movement 142
Craft Beer's Influence on Beer Culture 147

Wordbook 152

Supplementary Materials 155

Introduction
The Resurgence of Craft Beer

In recent decades, the world of beer has experienced a remarkable renaissance, redefining the beverage from a simple commodity into a cultural and artisanal phenomenon. This resurgence, known as the "Craft Beer Revolution," has transformed the beer landscape, rejuvenated ancient brewing traditions, and ignited a passion for beer that transcends the mere act of consumption. This chapter will explore the factors that contributed to the resurgence of craft beer, the driving forces behind its popularity, and the profound impact it has had on the beer industry and beer culture as a whole.

A New Era Dawns

The story of craft beer's resurgence is one of resilience, innovation, and a return to the roots of brewing. In the latter half of the 20th century, the beer industry had become dominated by a handful of corporate giants producing mass-produced lagers. This era of industrialization led to a homogenization of beer styles, with flavor taking a backseat to efficiency and cost-effectiveness. However, a growing dissatisfaction with the blandness of mainstream beers paved the way for a remarkable change.

The Pioneers of Craft

At the heart of the craft beer resurgence were a group of visionary brewers who dared to challenge the status quo. These pioneers, often referred to as the "Founding Fathers of

Craft Beer," were passionate about brewing and dedicated to producing high-quality, flavorful beers. Names like Fritz Maytag of Anchor Brewing, Ken Grossman of Sierra Nevada, and Jim Koch of Boston Beer Company (Samuel Adams) became synonymous with the craft beer movement. Their commitment to brewing excellence and their willingness to experiment with new ingredients and styles laid the foundation for the resurgence we witness today.

The Quest for Flavor and Diversity

Craft beer enthusiasts were seeking something more than the bland, watery offerings of mainstream beer. They craved flavor, complexity, and variety. Craft brewers responded by embracing a wide range of styles, from hoppy India Pale Ales (IPAs) to rich stouts and sours. This embrace of diverse beer styles not only satisfied the palates of beer enthusiasts but also fueled a spirit of creativity and experimentation within the industry.

Localism and Community

One of the defining characteristics of the craft beer resurgence was a return to localism and community. Craft breweries sprang up in neighborhoods across the country, offering unique flavors and experiences that were deeply tied to their geographic roots. These breweries weren't just places to buy beer; they became gathering spots, fostering a sense of community and camaraderie among patrons. The "drink local" movement took hold, encouraging consumers to support their neighborhood breweries.

A Cultural Shift

The resurgence of craft beer also brought about a cultural shift in how beer was perceived. It was no longer seen as a simple thirst-quencher but as a beverage that could be savored and explored, much like wine. Beer became a topic of conversation, a hobby, and even a form of art. This cultural shift elevated beer to new heights, with beer pairings, tasting events, and beer appreciation courses becoming commonplace.

A Global Movement

While the craft beer resurgence was most pronounced in the United States, it quickly spread worldwide. Craft breweries began to emerge in Europe, Asia, and beyond, each adding their unique twists to traditional brewing styles. The global craft beer movement not only celebrated diversity but also connected beer enthusiasts across borders, creating a worldwide community of beer lovers.

Conclusion

The resurgence of craft beer represents a remarkable chapter in the history of brewing. It is a story of passion, creativity, and a desire for authenticity in an increasingly industrialized world. In the chapters that follow, we will delve deeper into the various facets of this craft beer renaissance, exploring the birth of microbreweries, the diversity of craft beer styles, the brewpub revolution, the fight for independence and authenticity, the impact on the beer industry, the art and science of craft brewing, and the vibrant culture and community that have blossomed around this beloved beverage. As we journey through these chapters, we will witness the craft beer movement's enduring influence and celebrate the vibrant and ever-evolving world of beer.

The Scope of This Book

As we embark on this journey through the history and evolution of beer, it's essential to define the scope of this book and the specific aspects of the craft beer story that we will explore in detail. While the world of beer is vast and multifaceted, this book will focus on several key themes and chapters to provide a comprehensive yet manageable exploration of the subject.

A Historical Odyssey

Our exploration begins in the distant past, where we trace the origins of beer in ancient civilizations like Mesopotamia and Egypt. We'll unravel the threads of history to uncover the early brewing techniques, ingredients, and cultural significance of beer in these societies. From there, we'll journey through the centuries, witnessing the evolution of beer as it spreads across the globe.

The Birth of Microbreweries

In Chapter 1, "The Birth of Microbreweries," we'll dive into the resurgence of craft beer, exploring the early days of microbrewing and the visionaries who laid the foundation for the movement. We'll delve into the techniques and innovations that set craft brewing apart, and we'll examine the profound impact of microbreweries on local economies.

Exploring Craft Beer Styles

Chapter 2, "Exploring Craft Beer Styles," takes us deep into the world of beer diversity. We'll dissect the various styles of craft beer, from ales to lagers and beyond.

Along the way, we'll explore the concept of hybrid styles and creative brewing, as well as the regional specialties that have emerged within the craft beer movement.

The Brewpub Revolution

Chapter 3, "The Brewpub Revolution," invites us to explore the emergence of brewpubs. We'll discover how brewpubs became a cornerstone of the craft beer movement, blurring the lines between brewing and dining. This chapter will also showcase successful brewpub models and the unique experiences they offer.

Independent Craft Brewers and the Fight for Authenticity

In Chapter 4, "Independent Craft Brewers and the Fight for Authenticity," we'll delve into the definition of craft beer and independence. We'll explore the role of organizations like the Craft Brewers Association and their efforts to promote authenticity. This chapter will shed light on the challenges faced by craft brewers in maintaining their independence.

The Craft Beer Boom and Its Impact on the Beer Industry

Chapter 5, "The Craft Beer Boom and Its Impact on the Beer Industry," examines the meteoric rise of the craft beer segment. We'll analyze how craft beer's popularity has influenced consumer preferences and forced large brewing conglomerates to respond. We'll also consider the broader impact on global beer trends.

The Art and Science of Craft Brewing

In Chapter 6, "The Art and Science of Craft Brewing," we'll explore the mastery of the brewing craft. This chapter will delve into the roles of ingredients in crafting unique beers, the creative processes involved in beer development, and the spirit of innovation and experimentation that drives the craft beer industry.

Craft Beer Culture and Community

Chapter 7, "Craft Beer Culture and Community," shifts our focus to the passionate beer enthusiasts and connoisseurs who have propelled the craft beer movement. We'll take a closer look at beer festivals and events, the role of online communities, and the vibrant social aspects that have emerged within craft beer culture.

Celebrating the Craft Beer Renaissance

In the concluding chapter, "Celebrating the Craft Beer Renaissance," we'll reflect on the journey we've taken through the world of beer. We'll celebrate the enduring influence of the craft beer movement and its ongoing evolution. This chapter will underscore how craft beer has left an indelible mark on beer culture, forever changing the way we perceive and enjoy this ancient beverage.

Throughout this book, we'll weave together historical narratives, personal stories, industry insights, and cultural observations to provide you with a rich and comprehensive understanding of the craft beer phenomenon. We'll explore the past, present, and future of beer, celebrating the craftsmanship, innovation, and community that make this beverage a cherished part of our global culture. So, let's raise a glass and begin our journey through the fascinating world of beer.

The Impact of Craft Beer on the Brewing Landscape

As we delve into the story of craft beer's resurgence, it's essential to understand the profound impact this movement has had on the brewing landscape. Craft beer has not only revitalized traditional brewing practices but has also left an indelible mark on the entire industry. In this chapter, we will explore the multifaceted influence of craft beer, from the way it has reshaped consumer preferences to the challenges it has posed to brewing conglomerates and the broader implications for the beer world.

A Shift in Consumer Preferences

Craft beer's resurgence brought about a seismic shift in consumer preferences. No longer satisfied with mass-produced, bland lagers, consumers began to seek out flavorful, artisanal brews. This shift is characterized by a demand for diverse beer styles, unique flavors, and a deeper appreciation for the craftsmanship that goes into brewing. Craft beer enthusiasts value quality over quantity and are willing to explore a wide range of beer styles, from hop-forward IPAs to complex barrel-aged ales.

The Decline of Mainstream Lagers

The rise of craft beer has coincided with a decline in the sales of mainstream lagers produced by brewing giants. The traditional beer landscape, once dominated by a few major players, now faces fierce competition from the ever-expanding craft beer market. This competition has forced the brewing industry to adapt, innovate, and reconsider its approach to brewing and marketing.

Big Beer's Response to the Craft Beer Boom

In response to the craft beer boom, large brewing conglomerates have taken various approaches to maintain their market share. Some have acquired craft breweries, attempting to tap into the growing craft market while others have launched their own craft-style brands. These strategies have blurred the lines between what is considered "craft" and led to debates within the beer community about the authenticity of such endeavors.

The Proliferation of Small and Independent Breweries

Craft beer's resurgence has fueled the proliferation of small, independent breweries. Across the United States and around the world, new breweries continue to emerge, each with its unique identity and approach to brewing. These small breweries contribute to local economies, promote innovation, and create a dynamic and competitive brewing landscape.

The Rise of Beer Tourism

Craft breweries have become destinations in their own right, giving rise to the phenomenon of beer tourism. Enthusiasts travel to explore brewery taprooms, sample unique brews, and immerse themselves in the brewing process. This trend has not only boosted local economies but has also fostered a sense of community among beer lovers.

A Global Craft Beer Movement

Craft beer's influence is not limited to a single region or country. The craft beer movement has gone global, with breweries in Europe, Asia, and beyond adopting the principles of craft brewing. This internationalization has led to cross-cultural exchanges, resulting in the fusion of traditional beer styles with innovative brewing techniques.

The Impact on Beer Culture

Beyond its influence on the industry, craft beer has significantly impacted beer culture itself. It has elevated beer from a casual beverage to a subject of deep appreciation and study. Beer enthusiasts attend tastings, pairing events, and beer education programs to expand their knowledge and palates. Beer has become a conversation starter, a hobby, and a form of art, enriching the cultural fabric of communities around the world.

Conclusion

The impact of craft beer on the brewing landscape cannot be overstated. This resurgence has reinvigorated brewing traditions, redefined consumer preferences, challenged industry giants, and created a global community of beer enthusiasts. As we continue our journey through the chapters of this book, we will delve deeper into the specific facets of craft beer's influence, from the birth of microbreweries to the art and science of craft brewing. Together, we will celebrate the enduring legacy of craft beer and its role in shaping the rich tapestry of the beer world.

Chapter 1: The Birth of Microbreweries
The Early Days of Microbrewing

In the annals of brewing history, the emergence of microbreweries marked a pivotal moment. These small, independent breweries would come to play a significant role in the craft beer revolution, challenging the dominance of industrial brewing giants and paving the way for a resurgence of brewing craftsmanship. In this chapter, we delve into the early days of microbrewing, exploring the humble beginnings, the passionate pioneers, and the driving forces that gave rise to this revolutionary movement.

The Spark of Rebellion

The roots of the microbrewing movement can be traced back to the late 20th century, a time when the brewing industry was increasingly characterized by consolidation and homogenization. Large brewing conglomerates dominated the market, churning out a limited range of beer styles. In the face of this brewing monotony, a spark of rebellion ignited among a group of visionary individuals.

The Visionaries

Central to the early days of microbrewing were the visionary individuals who dared to challenge the status quo. These pioneers, often referred to as the "Founding Fathers of Craft Beer," were fueled by a passion for brewing and a desire to create beers of exceptional quality and character. Names like Fritz Maytag of Anchor Brewing, Jack McAuliffe of New Albion Brewing, and Ken Grossman of Sierra Nevada Brewing became synonymous with this new movement.

The Revival of Traditional Brewing Methods

One of the defining characteristics of the early microbrewing era was a return to traditional brewing methods. These brewers sought inspiration in historical brewing practices, often eschewing the modern shortcuts and additives used by their industrial counterparts. They championed all-grain brewing, natural ingredients, and time-honored techniques to create beers that paid homage to brewing's rich heritage.

A Commitment to Quality

Quality was paramount for these early microbrewers. They were committed to producing beers that met the highest standards of taste and craftsmanship. Each batch was crafted with meticulous attention to detail, ensuring that every bottle or keg delivered a unique and exceptional drinking experience.

A Focus on Flavor and Diversity

At the heart of the microbrewing movement was a passion for flavor and diversity. These early microbrewers rejected the notion that beer should be uniform and unadventurous. Instead, they embraced a wide range of beer styles, from the hoppy bitterness of India Pale Ales (IPAs) to the rich complexity of stouts and porters. This embrace of diversity not only satisfied the palates of beer enthusiasts but also encouraged experimentation and innovation.

Brewing Beyond Borders

As the movement gained momentum, it transcended geographical boundaries. Breweries small in scale but big in ambition began to sprout up across the United States. Each of these breweries offered its unique interpretation of beer styles, often influenced by the local culture and ingredients. This geographic diversity added depth and character to the growing world of microbrewing.

Grassroots Brewing

The early days of microbrewing were characterized by grassroots efforts and a do-it-yourself ethos. Many of these small breweries operated on shoestring budgets, with brewers taking on multiple roles, from brewing to packaging and distribution. This hands-on approach fostered a close connection between brewers and their craft.

The Impact of Microbreweries on Local Economies

Beyond their role in beer culture, microbreweries had a significant impact on local economies. They provided employment opportunities, revitalized neighborhoods, and contributed to the cultural identity of their communities. The "drink local" movement began to take shape, encouraging consumers to support their neighborhood breweries and embrace the concept of "community beer."

Conclusion

The early days of microbrewing laid the foundation for a movement that would redefine the brewing landscape. These pioneers, driven by their passion for beer and a commitment to quality, ignited a revolution that continues to shape the beer industry today. In the chapters that follow, we will delve deeper into the techniques and innovations that set microbrewing apart, explore the impact of microbreweries on local economies, and celebrate the enduring legacy of these trailblazers. The story of microbrewing is a testament to the transformative power of passion and creativity in the world of beer.

The Founding Fathers of Craft Beer

In the annals of brewing history, a group of pioneering individuals emerged as trailblazers in the craft beer revolution. These visionary brewers, often referred to as the "Founding Fathers of Craft Beer," played a pivotal role in shaping the early days of microbrewing and laying the foundation for the craft beer movement we know today. In this chapter, we delve into the lives, stories, and contributions of these passionate individuals who ignited the spark of craft beer's resurgence.

Fritz Maytag: Anchor Brewing Company

Fritz Maytag, scion of the Maytag appliance dynasty, is often credited as one of the foremost Founding Fathers of Craft Beer. In the late 1960s, Maytag rescued San Francisco's Anchor Brewing Company from near-closure. With unwavering dedication, he revitalized Anchor Steam Beer, a classic American steam beer style, and brought it back to prominence. Maytag's commitment to preserving traditional brewing methods and crafting beer with character set the stage for the craft beer movement.

Jack McAuliffe: New Albion Brewing Company

Jack McAuliffe is hailed as a true pioneer of the craft beer renaissance. In 1976, he founded New Albion Brewing Company in Sonoma, California, becoming one of the first small breweries in the United States since Prohibition. McAuliffe's determination to brew flavorful, small-batch beers against the backdrop of a brewing industry dominated by giants was nothing short of revolutionary. His legacy as a trailblazer inspired countless others to follow in his footsteps.

Ken Grossman: Sierra Nevada Brewing Company

Ken Grossman's journey in brewing began with a passion for homebrewing and a desire to create exceptional beer. In 1980, he co-founded Sierra Nevada Brewing Company in Chico, California. Sierra Nevada Pale Ale, one of the brewery's flagship beers, became an iconic brew and helped define the American craft beer style. Grossman's commitment to quality, use of whole-cone hops, and dedication to sustainable brewing practices set new standards for craft breweries.

Jim Koch: Boston Beer Company (Samuel Adams)

Jim Koch, founder of Boston Beer Company and creator of Samuel Adams Boston Lager, is another luminary in the world of craft beer. In 1984, Koch introduced Samuel Adams to the market, challenging the notion that only light, mass-produced lagers could succeed. Koch's tireless promotion of craft beer and his unwavering commitment to brewing excellence played a pivotal role in the craft beer movement's growth.

Other Influential Pioneers

While Fritz Maytag, Jack McAuliffe, Ken Grossman, and Jim Koch are often cited as some of the foremost Founding Fathers of Craft Beer, it's important to acknowledge that many other influential pioneers contributed to the movement's early success. Brewers like Charlie Papazian, founder of the American Homebrewers Association, and Michael Jackson, the renowned beer writer, helped popularize craft beer and educate consumers about its diversity and heritage.

A Shared Vision

What united these Founding Fathers was a shared vision—a vision of brewing beer that was more than just a commodity. They saw beer as an art form, an expression of creativity, and a product that deserved respect and attention to detail. Their passion for brewing, combined with their entrepreneurial spirit, paved the way for a craft beer movement that celebrated quality, diversity, and authenticity.

Legacy and Influence

The legacy of the Founding Fathers of Craft Beer extends far beyond their individual breweries. Their pioneering spirit and dedication to brewing excellence served as an inspiration to countless aspiring brewers who followed in their footsteps. Today, their influence can be seen in the thriving craft beer industry, where innovation and quality continue to be at the forefront.

Conclusion

The Founding Fathers of Craft Beer were not merely brewers; they were visionaries who reshaped the beer landscape. Their commitment to quality, their embrace of diverse beer styles, and their determination to revive traditional brewing methods laid the foundation for a movement that has reinvigorated the world of beer. As we explore the journey of microbreweries and the craft beer movement in this chapter and throughout this book, we pay tribute to these trailblazers who turned a passion for beer into a revolution. Their stories serve as a reminder of the transformative power of dedication, creativity, and a love for great beer.

Microbrewing Techniques and Innovation

In the early days of the microbrewing movement, brewers faced a unique set of challenges and opportunities. The shift towards small-scale, independent brewing demanded a departure from the mass production techniques employed by industrial brewing giants. In this chapter, we explore the microbrewing techniques and innovations that emerged during this transformative period, highlighting the creative approaches taken by pioneering brewers to craft distinctive and high-quality beers.

Small-Scale Brewing: The Heart of Microbrewing

At the core of microbrewing was the concept of small-scale production. Unlike industrial breweries that focused on large batch sizes for cost efficiency, microbrewers embraced the art of crafting beer in smaller quantities. This shift allowed for greater control over the brewing process and the ability to experiment with different ingredients and recipes.

All-Grain Brewing: Crafting from Scratch

Many early microbrewers adopted the practice of all-grain brewing, a traditional method that involves mashing malted barley and other grains to extract sugars for fermentation. All-grain brewing offered greater flexibility and the opportunity to create a wide range of beer styles, from malty lagers to hoppy ales. This departure from extract brewing marked a return to brewing's roots and elevated the quality and flavor of craft beers.

Ingredient Selection and Quality

Innovation in microbrewing extended to the selection and quality of ingredients. Brewers sought out the finest malted grains, hops, yeast strains, and water sources to create distinctive flavor profiles. Experimentation with diverse hop varieties, specialty malts, and unique adjuncts allowed for the creation of beers with complex and unique taste experiences.

Hop Forward: The Rise of the American IPA

The American India Pale Ale (IPA) emerged as an iconic style that exemplified microbrewing innovation. Craft brewers, influenced by traditional English IPAs, took this style to new heights by showcasing bold hop flavors and aromas. The use of American hop varieties like Cascade and Centennial created a signature hop-forward profile that became synonymous with the craft beer movement.

Crafting Unique and Specialty Beers

Microbrewers were not bound by tradition or convention. Their willingness to push boundaries led to the creation of specialty and experimental beers. From barrel-aged brews to sour ales, brewers explored uncharted territory, allowing for the development of diverse and adventurous beer styles that captivated the palates of beer enthusiasts.

Small Batches, Big Experimentation

The small batch sizes of microbreweries provided the ideal environment for experimentation. Brewers could test new recipes, yeast strains, and flavor combinations without the risk associated with large-scale production. This culture of experimentation led to the discovery of unique flavor profiles and the development of innovative brewing techniques.

Barrel Aging and Blending

The use of barrels for aging beer became a hallmark of craft brewing. Brewers embraced barrels that had previously housed spirits like whiskey, wine, or rum to impart unique flavors and complexities to their beers. Barrel aging and blending techniques allowed for the creation of rich, nuanced brews that pushed the boundaries of traditional beer styles.

Quality Control and Consistency

While innovation and experimentation were celebrated, craft brewers were also committed to quality control and consistency. Implementing rigorous quality assurance processes ensured that each batch of beer met the high standards set by the brewery. This dedication to quality helped build trust among consumers and contributed to the craft beer movement's reputation for excellence.

Sustainability and Brewing Practices

Innovative approaches extended beyond flavor profiles to brewing practices. Many craft brewers embraced sustainable and environmentally responsible methods, such as recycling, waste reduction, and energy efficiency. These practices not only aligned with the ethos of the craft beer movement but also reflected a commitment to responsible stewardship of resources.

Conclusion

Microbrewing techniques and innovation were integral to the success of the craft beer movement. The willingness of brewers to experiment, the embrace of all-grain brewing, and the focus on ingredient quality allowed for the creation of a diverse and exciting array of beers. In this chapter, we have explored how the craft beer pioneers leveraged their creativity, technical expertise, and dedication to quality to shape the brewing landscape, setting the stage for the flourishing world of craft beer that we celebrate today. As we continue our journey through the chapters of this book, we will uncover even more facets of the craft beer resurgence, from the impact on local economies to the unique beer styles that have emerged from this era of innovation and creativity.

The Impact of Microbreweries on Local Economies

As the craft beer movement began to take shape with the birth of microbreweries, it brought about not only a transformation in the beer industry but also a significant impact on local economies. In this chapter, we delve into the economic influence of microbreweries on their surrounding communities, exploring how these small, independent breweries became catalysts for growth, job creation, tourism, and revitalization.

Breweries as Economic Engines

Microbreweries, by their very nature, operate on a smaller scale compared to their industrial counterparts. However, their impact on local economies can be substantial. One of the primary ways in which microbreweries contribute to their communities is through job creation. They employ a range of skilled workers, from brewers and cellar operators to marketing and sales personnel, bolstering local employment opportunities.

The Power of the Local Supply Chain

Microbreweries often prioritize sourcing ingredients locally whenever possible. This approach extends beyond mere preference; it strengthens the local agricultural sector by creating a consistent demand for malt, hops, and other brewing ingredients. In turn, this support for local farmers and suppliers has a positive ripple effect on regional economies.

Brewpubs: Dining and Drinking Destinations

The emergence of brewpubs, which combine brewing facilities with a restaurant or pub, has further boosted the economic impact of microbreweries. Brewpubs become destinations for both locals and tourists, drawing in patrons not only for their beer offerings but also for their food menus. This dual appeal enhances the economic viability of these establishments and helps drive culinary tourism.

Tourism and Destination Brewing

Microbreweries have become tourist attractions in their own right. Visitors from near and far are drawn to the unique experiences that breweries offer, including brewery tours, tastings, and special events. This influx of tourists injects revenue into local economies, benefiting restaurants, hotels, and other businesses in the vicinity of the breweries.

Neighborhood Revitalization

The establishment of a microbrewery can be a catalyst for neighborhood revitalization. Many microbreweries set up shop in previously neglected or underutilized urban areas, breathing new life into these neighborhoods. Their presence often leads to increased foot traffic, which, in turn, can stimulate the growth of local businesses and property values.

The "Drink Local" Movement

The "drink local" movement, championed by microbreweries, encourages consumers to support nearby breweries and enjoy beers crafted within their communities. This movement promotes a sense of local pride and identity, fostering a stronger connection between residents and their local businesses.

Collaborations and Partnerships

Microbreweries frequently collaborate with neighboring businesses, creating synergistic partnerships that benefit both parties. Collaborative brews, joint marketing efforts, and cross-promotions further stimulate local economic activity and draw attention to the unique offerings of each partner.

The Tax Revenue Impact

Microbreweries contribute to tax revenue at various levels of government, from local to state and federal. The tax revenue generated by the sale of alcoholic beverages supports public services and infrastructure improvements, providing a direct benefit to the communities where microbreweries operate.

Challenges and Considerations

While microbreweries bring substantial economic benefits to their communities, they also face challenges, including zoning regulations, licensing, and competition from larger breweries. Managing growth while maintaining the essence of a small, independent brewery can be a delicate balancing act for microbrewers.

Conclusion

The impact of microbreweries on local economies extends far beyond the production of beer. These small, independent breweries have become integral parts of their communities, driving economic growth, creating jobs, and contributing to the cultural and culinary fabric of their regions. As we continue our exploration of the craft beer movement in the following chapters, we will uncover additional facets of this resurgence, from the fight for independence and authenticity to the global influence of craft beer. The story of microbreweries is not only about brewing exceptional beer but also about the positive economic transformation they bring to the neighborhoods and towns they call home.

Chapter 2: Exploring Craft Beer Styles
The Diversity of Craft Beer

Craft beer is a world of flavors, a spectrum of aromas, and a celebration of diversity. In this chapter, we embark on a journey through the diverse landscape of craft beer styles, each offering a unique taste experience. From hoppy ales to rich stouts, from traditional lagers to innovative hybrids, we explore the vast array of beer styles that have captivated the palates of enthusiasts and shaped the craft beer movement.

A Multitude of Styles

The hallmark of the craft beer movement is its embrace of a multitude of beer styles. Unlike the limited range of styles offered by industrial breweries, craft brewers revel in the opportunity to experiment with diverse ingredients and techniques. The result is an expansive menu of styles that cater to a wide range of tastes and preferences.

The World of Ales

Ales represent one of the largest and most diverse categories in the craft beer universe. Within this category, we encounter a spectrum of flavors and aromas, from the citrusy and piney notes of American Pale Ales (APAs) to the robust roastiness of Imperial Stouts. Exploring ales allows us to delve into the rich tapestry of hop varieties, yeast strains, and malt profiles that contribute to the diversity of craft beer.

Lagers: Tradition and Innovation

Lagers, long associated with crisp and clean beer profiles, are not immune to the craft beer revolution. Craft brewers have breathed new life into lagers, introducing innovative twists on classic styles. Pilsners, Helles, and Bocks are just a few examples of lager styles that have been reimagined by craft brewers, resulting in beers that are both refreshing and full of character.

The IPA Renaissance

The India Pale Ale (IPA) has become emblematic of the craft beer movement. This style has undergone a renaissance, with brewers experimenting with hop varieties from around the world to create a wide range of IPAs. From West Coast IPAs with their bold bitterness to New England IPAs known for their hazy appearance and juicy flavors, the IPA category showcases the versatility of hops and the creativity of brewers.

Sours and Wild Ales

Sour beers and wild ales represent a category of craft beer that challenges traditional notions of taste. These beers are characterized by acidity, tartness, and complex microbial fermentation. The use of wild yeast strains and bacteria results in beers that range from mildly tangy to intensely sour, offering a unique and adventurous drinking experience.

Stout and Porter: Dark and Delicious

Stouts and porters are beloved for their dark, roasted flavors, often accompanied by notes of chocolate, coffee, and caramel. These styles include classics like Dry Stout,

Imperial Stout, and Baltic Porter, each offering a different take on the dark beer experience. Craft brewers have elevated these styles to new heights with barrel aging, adding layers of complexity and depth.

Creative Hybrids and Adjuncts

The craft beer world is a playground for creativity. Brewers continually experiment with hybrid styles and adjuncts, pushing the boundaries of what beer can be. From the fusion of beer and wine in barrel-aged blends to the incorporation of unconventional ingredients like fruit, spices, and even candy, craft brewers delight in crafting beers that surprise and delight.

Regional Specialties

Craft beer is also about celebrating local traditions and ingredients. Breweries across the world draw inspiration from their regions to create unique and distinctive styles. We explore regional specialties like Belgian Trappist ales, German Kölsch, and American Cream Ales, each a reflection of its geographic and cultural context.

The Quest for Balance

While craft beer offers a wide spectrum of flavors, brewers also strive for balance. Achieving harmony among ingredients—malts, hops, yeast, and adjuncts—is a hallmark of craftsmanship. This quest for balance ensures that even the most flavorful beers are enjoyable and drinkable.

Conclusion

The diversity of craft beer styles is a testament to the creativity, innovation, and passion of brewers worldwide. In this chapter, we have only scratched the surface of the multifaceted world of craft beer. As we continue our exploration of the craft beer movement in the following chapters, we will delve deeper into the history and characteristics of specific styles, exploring the stories and traditions that make each one unique. Craft beer is a celebration of flavor, culture, and community, and its diversity is a testament to the enduring appeal of this beloved beverage.

Ales, Lagers, and Beyond

Craft beer is a realm of endless possibilities, and at its core lie two fundamental categories: ales and lagers. But within these broad classifications, a world of flavors, aromas, and experiences awaits. In this chapter, we embark on a journey through the diverse spectrum of ales, lagers, and other unique beer styles, each telling its own story and captivating the palates of beer enthusiasts.

Ales: A World of Diversity

Ales encompass a vast and diverse array of beer styles, each distinguished by its yeast, fermentation temperature, and ingredient profile. As we explore the world of ales, we encounter a tapestry of flavors and aromas that reflect the creativity and passion of craft brewers.

Pale Ales: A Hoppy Beginning

Pale ales, known for their balanced malt and hop profiles, have been redefined by the craft beer movement. American Pale Ales (APAs) offer a showcase of American hop varieties, with notes of citrus, pine, and floral characteristics. British Bitters, on the other hand, exhibit a more subdued hop presence, emphasizing malty sweetness and balance.

India Pale Ales (IPAs): A Bitter Revolution

IPAs have become the poster child of the craft beer movement. Craft brewers have breathed new life into this style, pushing the boundaries of hop bitterness and aroma. From West Coast IPAs with their crisp bitterness to New England IPAs (NEIPAs) with their hazy appearance and juicy, tropical fruit flavors, IPAs offer a diverse and dynamic range of taste experiences.

Imperial and Double IPAs: Bold and Robust

Imperial IPAs, often referred to as Double IPAs (DIPAs), take the hoppy intensity of IPAs to the next level. These high-alcohol brews showcase bold hop profiles with elevated malt sweetness, resulting in a robust and flavorful beer. Their strength makes them ideal for aging and experimentation.

Belgian Ales: Yeast-Driven Excellence

Belgian ales are renowned for their expressive yeast strains, which produce a wide range of fruity, spicy, and complex flavors. Styles like Belgian Dubbels, Tripels, and Quads offer a rich tapestry of flavors, often accompanied by higher alcohol content. Trappist ales, brewed by monks within monastic walls, are revered for their authenticity and dedication to tradition.

Sour Ales: A Tangy Adventure

Sour ales and wild ales challenge conventional beer flavors with their acidity and complexity. These beers undergo spontaneous or controlled fermentation with wild yeast strains and bacteria, resulting in a spectrum of tartness. From Berliner Weisse to Lambics and Goses, sour ales offer adventurous and refreshing taste experiences.

Lagers: Tradition and Innovation

Lagers, known for their clean and crisp profiles, have also seen a resurgence in the craft beer movement. Craft brewers honor lager traditions while infusing innovation to create lagers that rival their ale counterparts in complexity and flavor.

Pilsners: Crisp and Classic

Pilsners are celebrated for their crispness, balance, and drinkability. Craft brewers have embraced this classic style, crafting both traditional Czech Pilsners and hop-forward American Pilsners. The result is a category of lagers that showcases the delicate interplay between malt and hops.

Bocks: Robust and Malty

Bocks are lagers known for their malt-forward character, often featuring rich caramel and toasty flavors. Styles like Traditional Bocks, Doppelbocks, and Eisbocks offer a spectrum of malt-driven experiences, from the smooth and moderately strong to the robust and potent.

Hybrid Styles: Innovation in Lagers

Craft brewers continually push the boundaries of lager brewing by experimenting with hybrid styles. India Pale Lagers (IPLs) combine the hoppy intensity of IPAs with the clean fermentation profile of lagers. Mexican-style lagers provide a refreshing and crisp backdrop for innovative flavors and adjuncts.

Beyond Ales and Lagers

The craft beer movement is not limited to ales and lagers. Brewers consistently explore uncharted territory, resulting in unique and innovative beer styles that captivate adventurous palates.

Stout and Porter: Dark and Complex

Stouts and porters are known for their dark and roasted flavors, often accompanied by notes of chocolate, coffee, and caramel. Craft brewers have elevated these styles with barrel aging and the addition of creative ingredients, offering a depth of flavor and complexity that defies tradition.

Wheat Beers: Light and Refreshing

Wheat beers, such as Hefeweizens and American Wheat Ales, offer a refreshing alternative with their light and cloudy appearance. These beers are prized for their gentle, fruity yeast esters and subtle spice notes.

Specialty and Experimental Beers: Pushing Boundaries

Craft brewers thrive on pushing the boundaries of what beer can be. Specialty and experimental beers encompass a broad category of brews, from fruit-infused sours to pastry stouts. These beers captivate the imagination and challenge preconceived notions of taste.

Conclusion

The world of craft beer is a celebration of diversity and innovation. From the rich tradition of ales and lagers to the bold experimentation with hybrid styles and unique ingredients, craft brewers have created a vibrant tapestry of beer flavors and experiences. As we continue our exploration of craft beer in the following chapters, we will delve into the stories and traditions behind specific styles, uncovering the unique characteristics and cultural significance of each

Hybrid Styles and Creative Brewing

In the world of craft beer, innovation knows no bounds. Brewers continually push the envelope, blurring the lines between traditional beer styles and forging new paths in creative brewing. In this chapter, we explore the exciting realm of hybrid beer styles and the innovative techniques that have given rise to unique and boundary-pushing brews.

The Creative Spirit of Craft Brewing

Craft brewers are artists and scientists, and their canvas is a fermenter filled with possibilities. The drive to experiment and create has led to the emergence of hybrid beer styles that defy convention and celebrate the inventive spirit of the craft beer movement.

India Pale Lagers (IPLs): A Marriage of Ales and Lagers

India Pale Lagers, or IPLs, represent a fusion of hoppy ales and clean lagers. Brewers combine the crisp, clean fermentation of lagers with the bold hop profiles typically associated with ales. The result is a refreshing and aromatic beer style that offers the best of both worlds.

Black IPAs: Dark and Hoppy

Black IPAs, also known as Cascadian Dark Ales, challenge the expectation that dark beers must be malty and roasted. These beers combine the hoppy bitterness of IPAs with dark malt character, resulting in a brew that's simultaneously rich and hop-forward.

Belgian IPA: A Harmonious Blend

Belgian IPAs take inspiration from both the hoppy intensity of American IPAs and the expressive yeast strains of Belgian ales. This style showcases fruity esters, spicy phenols, and a vibrant hop presence, creating a harmonious fusion of flavors.

Sour IPAs: Tangy and Hoppy

Sour IPAs combine the tartness of sour ales with the hoppy character of IPAs. These beers feature a complex interplay of flavors, with sourness complementing the fruity and citrusy notes of hops.

Fruit IPAs: A Burst of Flavor

Fruit-infused IPAs are a testament to the creativity of craft brewers. These beers incorporate a variety of fruits, from citrus to tropical varieties, to enhance the hop and malt profile, resulting in a delightful burst of fruity flavors.

Spiced and Specialty Ales: Creative Ingredients

Craft brewers often experiment with spices, herbs, and unconventional ingredients to craft specialty ales that push the boundaries of traditional styles. From pumpkin ales with seasonal spices to chili-infused stouts, these brews are a celebration of creativity and flavor exploration.

Barrel-Aged Wonders: Complex Aging

Barrel aging has become an art form in itself, with brewers using a wide array of barrels, including those that previously held bourbon, wine, and spirits, to impart unique flavors to their beers. Barrel-aged beers often boast complex layers of oak, vanilla, and the residual flavors from their former occupants.

Mixed Fermentation: Blending Tradition and Modernity

Mixed fermentation beers combine the age-old practice of blending beer from different batches with modern brewing techniques. Brewers create intricate and layered brews by mixing various aged and young beers, resulting in nuanced flavors and aromas.

Pastry Stouts and Dessert Beers: Sweet Indulgence

Pastry stouts and dessert beers take inspiration from sweet treats, incorporating ingredients like chocolate, vanilla, coffee, and even pastry dough. These indulgent brews offer a rich and dessert-like experience, satisfying those with a sweet tooth.

Collaborative Brewing: Sharing Ideas and Expertise

Craft brewers often collaborate with other breweries, both locally and internationally, to create unique and limited-edition beers. These collaborations foster a spirit of camaraderie, allowing brewers to share ideas, techniques, and ingredients.

Sustainability in Brewing: Creative Responsibility

Innovation in craft brewing extends to sustainability. Brewers explore eco-friendly practices, from recycling brewing byproducts to utilizing solar energy, as they strive to minimize their environmental footprint while continuing to create exceptional beers.

Conclusion

The world of craft beer is a testament to the boundless creativity of brewers. Hybrid styles and creative brewing techniques have expanded the horizons of beer, challenging conventions and offering beer enthusiasts a diverse and dynamic range of flavors and experiences. In the following chapters, we will delve deeper into specific styles and explore the rich history and cultural significance of each, providing a comprehensive view of the craft beer movement and the impact it has had on beer culture around the world.

Regional Craft Beer Specialties

Craft beer is a tapestry woven from diverse threads, and one of its most captivating aspects is the influence of regional traditions and ingredients. In this chapter, we embark on a journey through the world of regional craft beer specialties, each a reflection of its geographic and cultural context. From Belgian Trappist ales to German lagers and American regional brews, we explore the rich tapestry of flavors that define beer traditions around the globe.

Belgian Trappist Ales: Monastic Excellence

Belgium is home to some of the world's most revered and historic beer styles, many of which are brewed within the walls of Trappist monasteries. These monastic breweries, known for their commitment to tradition and quality, produce a range of beer styles, including Dubbels, Tripels, and Quadrupels. Each of these beers is characterized by rich malt sweetness, fruity yeast esters, and a complexity that deepens with age.

The Trappist Tradition: A Legacy of Brewing

Trappist monks have been brewing beer for centuries, not only to sustain their communities but also to support charitable endeavors. We explore the history and traditions of Trappist brewing, highlighting the dedication to authenticity and craftsmanship that defines these beers.

German Lagers: Purity and Precision

Germany is synonymous with lagers, and its brewing traditions are steeped in purity laws and precise craftsmanship. From the crisp and refreshing Pilsners of the Czech-influenced regions to the malty richness of Bocks and Doppelbocks, German lagers offer a spectrum of flavors that reflect both tradition and innovation.

Reinheitsgebot: The Purity Law

The Reinheitsgebot, or German Beer Purity Law, has shaped the brewing culture of Germany for centuries. We delve into the history and significance of this law, which dictates the ingredients that can be used in beer production and has helped maintain the country's reputation for quality brewing.

English Ales: From Bitters to Stouts

England has a rich tradition of brewing ales, ranging from the sessionable and moderately bitter Bitters to the robust and dark Stouts. These beers reflect the country's love of pub culture and its appreciation for nuanced, malt-forward flavors.

Cask Ale: A Unique Tradition

Cask ale, also known as real ale, is a distinctive British tradition that involves natural fermentation in casks and cellar temperature serving. We explore the history of cask ale and its enduring popularity among beer enthusiasts.

Czech Pilsners: The Original Pale Lager

The Czech Republic gave birth to the Pilsner style, known for its golden clarity and balanced bitterness. Pilsner Urquell, the world's first pale lager, remains a testament to the country's brewing prowess.

Pilsner Urquell: A Historical Brew

Pilsner Urquell's story is one of innovation and pioneering brewing techniques. We explore the history and significance of this iconic beer, which set the stage for the global popularity of pale lagers.

American Regional Brews: A Tapestry of Styles

The United States has embraced the craft beer movement with open arms, resulting in a flourishing of regional beer specialties. From West Coast IPAs to New England Hazy IPAs, and from Kentucky Bourbon Barrel Ales to Pacific Northwest Cascadian Dark Ales, we explore how American craft brewers have put their unique stamp on beer styles.

West Coast vs. East Coast IPAs

The West Coast IPA and New England IPA represent two distinct approaches to the same style. We delve into the differences in appearance, aroma, and flavor that define these regional variations.

International Influences: Fusion and Fusion Beers

Globalization has led to cross-cultural influences in brewing. We explore fusion beers that blend elements from different beer cultures, such as Japanese Saisons, Mexican-style lagers, and Belgian-inspired American brews.

Local Ingredients: Terroir and Taste

Craft brewers increasingly emphasize locally sourced ingredients to create beers that reflect their region's terroir. From Pacific Northwest hops to Appalachian grains, we examine how local ingredients contribute to regional beer specialties.

Conclusion

The world of regional craft beer specialties is a testament to the enduring allure of beer as a reflection of culture, tradition, and place. As we continue our exploration of the craft beer movement in the following chapters, we will delve into the stories, histories, and cultural significance of specific styles, uncovering the unique characteristics that make each one a cherished part of the global beer landscape. Craft beer is a celebration of diversity and a testament to the bonds between people and their local traditions, and it continues to captivate palates and cultures worldwide.

Chapter 3: The Brewpub Revolution
The Emergence of Brewpubs

The craft beer movement didn't just change what we drink; it transformed how and where we enjoy our beer. In this chapter, we delve into the emergence of brewpubs, a pivotal aspect of the craft beer renaissance. Brewpubs represent a fusion of brewing and hospitality, creating vibrant spaces where beer lovers can savor freshly brewed beers while enjoying a unique dining experience.

The Birth of the Brewpub Concept

The brewpub concept began to take shape in the late 20th century as a response to the growing interest in craft beer. It represented a departure from traditional bars and taverns, offering patrons not only a place to drink but also a direct connection to the brewing process.

Key Pioneers: Anchor Brewing and New Albion

We explore the early pioneers of the brewpub movement, including Anchor Brewing in San Francisco and New Albion Brewing in California. These breweries played a crucial role in popularizing the idea of brewing and serving beer on-site.

Defining Brewpubs: Brewery + Pub

A brewpub is more than just a place that brews and serves its own beer; it's a holistic experience that combines elements of a brewery and a pub. We examine the key characteristics that define brewpubs, from in-house brewing equipment to a welcoming pub atmosphere.

The Craft of Brewing and Hospitality

Brewpubs celebrate both the craft of brewing and the art of hospitality. Brewers have the opportunity to experiment with recipes and styles, often brewing small-batch and specialty beers that are exclusive to their establishment. Meanwhile, chefs work alongside brewers to create food menus that complement the beers, offering patrons a complete dining experience.

Brewpub Locations: Urban Revitalization

Many brewpubs are strategically located in urban areas, contributing to the revitalization of neighborhoods and downtown districts. We explore how brewpubs have breathed new life into once-neglected areas, drawing in visitors and fostering economic growth.

Brewpub Architecture and Ambiance

The design and ambiance of brewpubs are carefully curated to provide a unique and welcoming atmosphere. We delve into the architectural elements and interior design that make brewpubs distinctive, from cozy taprooms with exposed brewing equipment to outdoor beer gardens.

The Role of the Brewer-Publican

Brewpubs are often helmed by brewer-publicans who are not only skilled brewers but also passionate about the experience they offer patrons. We profile some of these brewer-publicans who have made a significant impact on the brewpub scene.

Brewery Tours and Education

Brewpubs are more than just places to drink and dine; they also serve as educational hubs for beer enthusiasts. Many brewpubs offer brewery tours and tastings, providing patrons with insights into the brewing process and beer culture.

Local Sourcing and Sustainability

Brewpubs often emphasize local sourcing, from ingredients to furnishings, contributing to sustainability and supporting nearby businesses. We explore how these establishments prioritize sustainability in their operations.

Brewpub Challenges: Balancing Art and Business

Running a successful brewpub involves balancing the artistic pursuit of brewing with the demands of running a business. We delve into the challenges that brewpub owners face, from managing inventory to navigating regulations.

Conclusion

The emergence of brewpubs represents a significant milestone in the craft beer revolution. These establishments have redefined the way we enjoy and appreciate beer, offering a dynamic fusion of brewing excellence and hospitality. As we continue our exploration of the brewpub revolution in the following chapters, we will delve deeper into the role of brewpubs in the craft beer movement, exploring their impact on the beer culture and the communities they serve. Brewpubs are not just places to enjoy beer; they are vibrant hubs that celebrate the craftsmanship and camaraderie of the craft beer world.

The Role of Brewpubs in the Craft Beer Movement

Brewpubs are more than just places to enjoy a pint of freshly brewed beer; they represent a vital and transformative aspect of the craft beer movement. In this chapter, we delve into the multifaceted role of brewpubs in shaping and driving the craft beer renaissance. From fostering innovation to nurturing community and expanding beer culture, brewpubs have played a pivotal role in the evolution of craft beer.

The Catalysts of Innovation

Brewpubs are often the laboratories of the craft beer world, where brewers have the freedom and creative license to experiment with ingredients, styles, and brewing techniques. We explore how brewpubs have driven innovation within the industry, introducing new flavors, styles, and approaches to brewing.

Small Batch Brewing: The Art of Experimentation

The relatively small scale of brewpub operations allows for nimble experimentation. Brewers can produce limited batches of experimental beers, pushing the boundaries of flavor and technique. We showcase examples of innovative brewpub creations.

Style Revival: Rediscovering Forgotten Styles

Brewpubs have been instrumental in resurrecting forgotten or obscure beer styles, breathing new life into traditional recipes that might have otherwise faded into obscurity. We examine how these establishments have contributed to style revivals.

Barrel Aging and Blending: Craftsmanship at its Finest

Brewpubs have pioneered barrel aging and blending techniques, elevating the craft to an art form. We explore how these establishments have mastered the use of barrels to create complex and nuanced beers.

Fostering Community and Connection

Brewpubs serve as focal points for community engagement and social interaction. These establishments provide spaces where beer enthusiasts can gather, share experiences, and connect with one another.

Local Gathering Spots: Neighborhood Hubs

Brewpubs often become beloved neighborhood gathering spots, fostering a sense of community and camaraderie. We share stories of brewpubs that have become cherished local institutions.

Beer Culture and Education

Brewpubs contribute to beer culture by offering educational experiences to patrons. Brewery tours, tastings, and beer education sessions provide opportunities for patrons to deepen their appreciation and knowledge of craft beer.

Events and Festivals: Celebrating Beer Together

Brewpubs frequently host events and beer festivals that celebrate the craft. These gatherings not only showcase their own beers but also promote collaboration and the sharing of beer culture with the wider community.

Craft Beer Tourism

Brewpubs are often destinations for craft beer enthusiasts and tourists alike. We explore how brewpubs have contributed to the growth of craft beer tourism, drawing visitors from near and far to experience their unique offerings.

Beer Travel: Exploring Regional Brewpub Scenes

Craft beer tourists often embark on journeys to explore regional brewpub scenes, visiting multiple establishments in pursuit of new and exciting beer experiences. We highlight some of the popular brewpub destinations around the world.

Culinary Tourism: Pairing Beer and Food

Many brewpubs offer exceptional food menus that complement their beer offerings. This culinary dimension adds an extra layer to the craft beer tourism experience, attracting food and beer enthusiasts alike.

Promoting Local and Sustainable Practices

Brewpubs often prioritize local sourcing of ingredients, sustainability, and environmentally responsible practices. We delve into how these establishments support local communities and contribute to a greener future.

Farm-to-Table: Local Sourcing

Brewpubs frequently collaborate with local farmers and suppliers to source fresh ingredients, creating a direct economic impact on their communities.

Sustainability Initiatives: Reducing Environmental Footprint

Many brewpubs are at the forefront of sustainability efforts in the brewing industry, implementing eco-friendly practices such as energy efficiency, waste reduction, and water conservation.

Challenges and Future Outlook

While brewpubs have thrived as dynamic hubs of beer culture, they also face challenges in an ever-evolving industry. We discuss the hurdles brewpubs encounter, from regulatory constraints to market competition, and explore strategies for their continued success.

Conclusion

Brewpubs are not just places to enjoy beer; they are vibrant and transformative entities within the craft beer movement. From fostering innovation and community to promoting sustainability and contributing to beer culture, brewpubs have left an indelible mark on the world of craft beer. As we continue our exploration of the brewpub revolution in the following chapters, we will delve deeper into the stories and traditions of specific brewpubs, uncovering the unique characteristics and cultural significance of each. Brewpubs are more than just venues;

they are living embodiments of the craft beer ethos, and they continue to shape the future of the industry.

The Experience of Brewing and Dining Together

Brewpubs offer a unique and immersive experience that goes beyond traditional dining or drinking establishments. In this chapter, we explore the captivating synergy between brewing and dining that defines brewpub culture. From witnessing the brewing process to savoring thoughtfully crafted beer and food pairings, brewpubs create a holistic and memorable experience for patrons.

Brewing as Theater

At brewpubs, brewing becomes a form of live theater. Patrons can witness the brewing process up close, from mashing in to boiling, fermenting, and packaging. This transparency fosters a sense of connection and authenticity, allowing beer enthusiasts to engage with the craft in a tangible way.

Open Brewing Areas: Transparency and Education

Many brewpubs feature open brewing areas or glass-enclosed brewing vessels, providing patrons with a view of the brewing process. We explore how this transparency enhances the brewpub experience and serves as an educational tool.

The Craft of Pairing: Beer and Food

One of the hallmarks of brewpub dining is the art of pairing beer with food. Brewpub chefs work closely with brewers to create menus that complement and enhance the flavors of the beer. We delve into the principles of beer and food pairing and highlight some exceptional brewpub pairings.

Flavor Synergy: Balancing Beer and Food

Brewpubs aim to create flavor harmony between beer and dishes. We explore how different beer styles can amplify or contrast with the flavors of various cuisines, resulting in a heightened dining experience.

Collaborative Menus: Chef and Brewer Partnerships

Brewpub chefs and brewers often collaborate closely to craft menus that incorporate beer into recipes or create dishes specifically designed to pair with particular brews. We share examples of these collaborative culinary endeavors.

Tasting Flights and Sampler Menus

Brewpubs often offer tasting flights or sampler menus that allow patrons to explore a variety of beer styles in one sitting. These options encourage experimentation and discovery, inviting patrons to expand their beer horizons.

Guided Tastings: Beer Education

Some brewpubs offer guided tastings led by knowledgeable staff or brewers. These sessions provide insights into the flavor profiles of different beers and offer an educational dimension to the brewpub experience.

Themed and Seasonal Menus

Brewpubs frequently create themed or seasonal menus that align with holidays, cultural events, or specific beer releases. We examine how these menus enhance the overall dining experience and create excitement among patrons.

Oktoberfest Celebrations: A Bavarian Tradition

Many brewpubs embrace the Oktoberfest tradition, offering a lineup of German-style lagers and hearty fare to celebrate the season. We explore how brewpubs capture the spirit of this iconic beer festival.

Special Beer Releases and Barrel-Aged Treats

Brewpubs often reserve special beers and barrel-aged treats for their patrons. These limited releases generate anticipation and reward loyal customers with unique and exceptional brews.

Barrel-Aged Dinners: A Culinary Affair

Some brewpubs host barrel-aged beer dinners, where patrons can savor carefully curated courses paired with aged and complex beers. These events offer an elevated dining experience.

The Role of Brewpub Staff

The staff at brewpubs play a crucial role in enhancing the overall experience. We examine the importance of knowledgeable and passionate servers, bartenders, brewers, and chefs in creating a memorable visit.

Beer Education: The Brewpub Team

Staff members often undergo training in beer styles, brewing techniques, and food pairings. Their expertise enhances patrons' understanding and appreciation of the beer and food offerings.

Community and Gatherings

Brewpubs serve as hubs for community gatherings, whether it's a casual meet-up with friends or a special event. We explore the role of brewpubs in fostering connections and social interactions.

Private Events: Celebrating Milestones

Brewpubs are popular venues for private events, including weddings, birthdays, and corporate gatherings. We share stories of memorable celebrations held at brewpubs.

Conclusion

The experience of brewing and dining together at brewpubs represents the pinnacle of craft beer enjoyment. From observing the brewing process to savoring thoughtfully paired beer and food, brewpubs create a holistic and immersive experience that engages the senses and fosters a sense of community. As we continue our exploration of the brewpub revolution in the following chapters, we will delve deeper into the stories and traditions of specific brewpubs, uncovering the unique characteristics and cultural significance of each. Brewpubs are not just places to eat and drink; they are vibrant spaces where the craft of brewing meets the art of hospitality, creating lasting memories for patrons.

Successful Brewpub Models

The brewpub landscape is as diverse as the craft beer styles it produces. In this chapter, we explore a range of successful brewpub models that have not only thrived but also played a significant role in shaping the brewpub revolution. From traditional brewpubs rooted in history to modern brewpub concepts that push boundaries, each model offers a unique perspective on what a brewpub can be.

The Classic Neighborhood Brewpub

The classic neighborhood brewpub embodies the essence of community. These establishments are often cozy and welcoming, with a focus on serving the local residents. We delve into the characteristics that define this model and share stories of iconic neighborhood brewpubs.

Local Loyalty: Building a Strong Customer Base

Neighborhood brewpubs often prioritize building strong relationships with their local patrons. We explore how this loyalty contributes to their sustained success.

Community Engagement: Beyond Beer

These brewpubs go beyond beer by actively participating in local events, supporting charitable causes, and fostering a sense of belonging in the neighborhood.

The Destination Brewpub

Destination brewpubs are located in tourist-friendly areas and attract visitors from near and far. We examine what makes these brewpubs special and the strategies they employ to draw in beer enthusiasts and tourists.

Scenic Settings: Location Matters

Many destination brewpubs are situated in picturesque locations, such as coastal towns, scenic mountain regions, or historic districts. We explore how the natural or cultural surroundings enhance the brewpub experience.

Events and Festivals: Drawing a Crowd

These brewpubs often host events and beer festivals that capitalize on their tourist appeal. We highlight some of the most popular destination brewpub events.

The Culinary Brewpub

Culinary brewpubs elevate the beer and food pairing experience to an art form. We examine how these establishments combine exceptional brewing with gourmet cuisine.

Renowned Chefs: Collaborations and Creations

Culinary brewpubs often attract renowned chefs who are passionate about incorporating beer into their culinary creations. We share examples of chef-brewer partnerships.

Beer Dinners: Elevated Pairing Experiences

Some culinary brewpubs host beer dinners that showcase meticulously crafted courses paired with a selection of brewpub beers. These events offer patrons a refined dining experience.

The Brewery Restaurant

Brewery restaurants seamlessly integrate brewing with fine dining. We explore how these models create a synergy between exceptional beer production and gourmet culinary offerings.

Brewery Showcases: On-Site Brewing Visibility

Brewery restaurants often have on-site brewing equipment that is visible to patrons. We discuss how this transparency enhances the overall experience.

Beer-Infused Cuisine: Creative Culinary Ventures

These establishments incorporate beer into various aspects of their cuisine, from beer-battered dishes to beer-infused sauces and desserts.

The Experimental Brewpub

Experimental brewpubs are at the forefront of innovation, pushing the boundaries of brewing with creative ingredients and techniques. We explore how these establishments balance tradition with bold experimentation.

Limited Releases: Exclusive Offerings

Experimental brewpubs often release limited and innovative beers that generate buzz among beer enthusiasts. We showcase some of the most unique and daring brewpub creations.

Barrel Aging and Blending: Mastery of Complexity

These brewpubs excel in barrel aging and blending, producing complex and sought-after beers that are often aged in wine or spirit barrels.

The Eco-Friendly Brewpub

Eco-friendly brewpubs prioritize sustainability in their operations, from sourcing local ingredients to implementing green initiatives. We discuss how these establishments contribute to environmental responsibility.

Sustainability Initiatives: Leading by Example

These brewpubs often set industry standards for sustainability, from energy-efficient equipment to waste reduction and water conservation.

Conclusion

Successful brewpub models are as diverse as the craft beer landscape itself. From classic neighborhood establishments that build strong local communities to destination brewpubs that draw in tourists, each model offers a unique perspective on what it means to be a brewpub. As we continue our exploration of the brewpub revolution in the following chapters, we will delve deeper into the stories and traditions of specific brewpubs, uncovering the unique characteristics and cultural significance of each. Brewpubs are not just places to enjoy beer; they are dynamic and multifaceted entities that celebrate the craft of brewing and the art of hospitality.

Chapter 4: Independent Craft Brewers and the Fight for Authenticity

Defining Craft Beer and Independence

The craft beer movement is defined not only by its diverse flavors but also by its commitment to authenticity and independence. In this chapter, we delve into the core principles that define craft beer and explore the ongoing fight for independence within the industry. From the early days of the craft beer renaissance to the present, the definition of "craft beer" has been a subject of debate and evolution.

The Birth of Craft Beer

To understand the definition of craft beer, we must first explore its origins. We take a journey back to the early days of the craft beer movement, examining how a handful of passionate brewers ignited a revolution.

Homebrewing Roots: A Grassroots Movement

Many craft brewers began as homebrewers, experimenting with small batches in garages and kitchens. We explore how this grassroots movement laid the foundation for the craft beer renaissance.

Pioneering Brewers: Visionaries of Flavor

The pioneering brewers who led the charge in the 1970s and 1980s had a shared vision: to challenge the status quo of bland, mass-produced beer. We highlight some of the key figures who played pivotal roles in the early days of craft beer.

The Craft Brewer's Declaration of Independence

Craft brewers have long been committed to producing beer that is independent, traditional, and innovative. We delve into the Brewers Association's Craft Brewer Definition and how it sets the standard for craft beer authenticity.

The Three Pillars: Independence, Traditional, and Small

The Brewers Association defines a craft brewer as one that is small, independent, and traditional. We examine each of these pillars and their significance in preserving the authenticity of craft beer.

The Independent Seal: A Mark of Authenticity

The Brewers Association introduced the Independent Craft Brewer Seal as a symbol of independence. We explore the role of this seal in helping consumers identify and support independent craft brewers.

The Seal's Impact: Consumer Awareness

The Independent Craft Brewer Seal empowers consumers to make informed choices and support small, independent breweries. We discuss its impact on consumer preferences.

Brewery Stories: Highlighting Independence

Breweries that meet the Brewers Association's criteria proudly display the Independent Craft Brewer Seal on their packaging and marketing materials. We share stories of breweries that wear the seal as a badge of honor.

Challenges to Independence

While craft brewers are committed to independence, they face challenges from various fronts, including acquisitions by large beer corporations. We examine the controversies surrounding brewery acquisitions and their impact on the perception of authenticity.

Brewery Buyouts: The Controversy

When large beer corporations acquire craft breweries, it can create tension within the industry. We explore the debates and discussions surrounding these buyouts.

Staying True to Craft: Independence vs. Growth

Some craft brewers face the dilemma of balancing their desire for growth with their commitment to independence. We discuss the challenges of maintaining authenticity while expanding operations.

Authenticity Beyond Definition

Authenticity in craft beer goes beyond a strict definition. It encompasses a dedication to quality, a connection to the community, and a passion for innovation. We explore how these elements contribute to the overall authenticity of craft beer.

Quality and Consistency: Craftsmanship Matters

Craft brewers take pride in the quality and consistency of their products. We delve into the meticulous craftsmanship that defines the authenticity of craft beer.

Community Engagement: Local Roots

Craft breweries often have strong ties to their communities, supporting local causes and collaborating with nearby businesses. We discuss how community engagement adds to the authenticity of craft beer.

Innovation and Creativity: The Spirit of Craft

Craft brewers continually push the boundaries of flavor, experimenting with ingredients and techniques. We explore how innovation and creativity are essential components of authenticity.

Conclusion

Defining craft beer and independence is an ongoing journey that reflects the ever-evolving nature of the craft beer movement. Craft brewers are committed to preserving the authenticity of their products while navigating challenges and opportunities in the industry. As we continue our exploration of independent craft brewers and their fight for authenticity in the following chapters, we will delve deeper into the stories and experiences of specific breweries, uncovering the unique characteristics that make each one a champion of craft beer's authentic spirit. Craft beer is more than just a beverage; it is a testament to the dedication, creativity, and independence of its brewers.

Craft Brewers Association and the Independent Seal

The Craft Brewers Association (CBA) and its Independent Craft Brewer Seal have become central figures in the craft beer industry, championing the values of independence, tradition, and authenticity. In this chapter, we explore the role of the CBA and the significance of the Independent Craft Brewer Seal in shaping the craft beer landscape and upholding the principles of the movement.

The Birth of the Craft Brewers Association

The Craft Brewers Association (CBA) emerged as a unifying force in the craft beer industry, bringing together independent brewers to advocate for their interests and promote craft beer as a whole. We delve into the history of the CBA and its mission.

A Collective Voice: Advocating for Brewers

The CBA was founded to provide a collective voice for independent craft brewers in the face of industry challenges and regulatory issues. We explore how the association represents the interests of its members.

The Brewers Association: An Expansive Network

The Brewers Association, a division of the CBA, is a multifaceted organization that encompasses brewing education, industry statistics, and beer events, in addition to advocating for craft brewers.

Defining Craft: The Brewers Association's Criteria

The Brewers Association established clear criteria to define what constitutes a craft brewer. We delve into the three pillars—small, independent, and traditional—that form the foundation of the craft brewer definition.

Small: Brewing at Scale

Craft brewers are defined as "small" based on their annual production. We discuss the specific production limits and why they are essential to the craft beer definition.

Independent: The Heart of Authenticity

Independence is at the core of the craft brewer definition, signifying ownership by a small, traditional brewer. We examine the significance of this pillar and how it contributes to the authenticity of craft beer.

Traditional: Honoring Brewing Heritage

Traditional practices are fundamental to craft brewing, emphasizing the use of traditional ingredients and brewing techniques. We explore the importance of preserving brewing heritage.

The Independent Craft Brewer Seal: A Symbol of Authenticity

The Independent Craft Brewer Seal was introduced by the Brewers Association to help consumers easily identify and support independent craft brewers. We delve into the creation and purpose of the seal.

The Seal's Design: A Mark of Pride

The Independent Craft Brewer Seal features a stylized beer bottle and is designed to be eye-catching and recognizable. We discuss the symbolism behind the design.

Educating Consumers: Empowering Choice

The seal empowers consumers to make informed choices when selecting beer. We explore how the seal serves as a tool for educating beer enthusiasts.

Seal Adoption and Impact

Breweries that meet the Brewers Association's criteria proudly display the Independent Craft Brewer Seal on their packaging, marketing materials, and taproom signage. We examine the adoption rates and the impact of the seal on consumer preferences.

Stories of Seal Adoption: Brewer Testimonials

We share stories and testimonials from craft brewers who have embraced the Independent Craft Brewer Seal and what it means to them and their customers.

Consumer Awareness: Recognizing Independence

The seal has raised consumer awareness about the importance of supporting independent craft brewers. We discuss how it has influenced purchasing decisions.

The Seal and Brewery Growth

Breweries often face the challenge of balancing their commitment to independence with their aspirations for growth. We explore how some breweries navigate this balance while proudly displaying the Independent Craft Brewer Seal.

Staying Independent: A Commitment to Values

Many breweries view independence as a fundamental value worth preserving, even as they expand their operations. We discuss the ways in which they stay true to their principles.

The Seal's Impact on Industry Dynamics

The Independent Craft Brewer Seal has not only empowered consumers but also influenced industry dynamics, including retailer and distributor relationships, and partnerships within the craft beer community. We examine these effects.

Conclusion

The Craft Brewers Association and the Independent Craft Brewer Seal have become symbols of authenticity and independence in the craft beer world. As we continue our exploration of independent craft brewers and their fight for authenticity in the following chapters, we will delve deeper into the stories and experiences of specific breweries that proudly wear the seal as a badge of honor. Craft beer is more than just a beverage; it is a testament to the dedication, creativity, and independence of its brewers, and the seal serves as a powerful reminder of those principles.

The Challenges of Staying Independent

While the craft beer movement is rooted in the values of independence and authenticity, staying true to these principles can be a challenging endeavor. In this chapter, we explore the various hurdles that independent craft brewers face as they strive to maintain their autonomy and uphold the craft beer ethos.

The Allure of Acquisition

One of the most significant challenges to independence comes in the form of acquisition offers from large beer corporations. We delve into the reasons behind these offers and the dilemmas they present to craft brewers.

Craft Brewery Acquisitions: A Controversial Trend

We examine the trend of craft brewery acquisitions by large beer corporations and the controversies that surround these buyouts.

The Temptation of Financial Security

For some craft brewers, acquisition offers promise financial stability and growth opportunities. We discuss the allure of financial security and what it means for the craft beer industry.

Balancing Growth and Independence

As craft breweries expand and increase production, they often grapple with the tension between growth and independence. We explore the challenges of scaling up while preserving the values of craft beer.

Production Challenges: Meeting Demand

Expanding production to meet growing demand requires substantial investments in equipment, facilities, and personnel. We discuss the complexities involved in scaling up.

Access to Market: Distribution and Shelf Space

Craft brewers need access to market channels and shelf space to reach consumers. We examine the challenges of competing with larger breweries for distribution and retail space.

Maintaining Quality: Consistency and Craftsmanship

Maintaining the quality and consistency of beer becomes increasingly challenging as production volumes grow. We explore the importance of quality control and craftsmanship.

Distribution and Shelf Space Battles

Craft brewers often face challenges when it comes to distribution and securing shelf space in a competitive marketplace. We delve into the complexities of distribution battles and the quest for visibility.

Distribution Agreements: Navigating Contracts

Craft brewers must negotiate distribution agreements that align with their goals and values. We discuss the intricacies of these agreements and their impact on independence.

Shelf Space Competition: The Retail Challenge

Securing prominent shelf space in retail stores is a constant battle. We examine how craft brewers vie for visibility alongside larger beer brands.

Maintaining Authenticity Amid Competition

As the craft beer market becomes increasingly crowded, craft brewers must find ways to differentiate themselves and maintain their authenticity. We explore strategies for standing out in a competitive landscape.

Innovation and Creativity: Brewing Uniqueness

Craft brewers rely on innovation and creativity to brew unique and exciting beers. We discuss how these traits set them apart from the competition.

Community Engagement: Local Roots

Craft breweries often foster strong ties with their communities. We examine how community engagement contributes to authenticity and loyalty.

The Role of Craft Beer Associations

Craft beer associations like the Brewers Association play a vital role in supporting independent craft brewers. We explore how these associations provide resources and advocacy for the craft beer industry.

Unity and Advocacy: Strength in Numbers

Craft beer associations advocate for the interests of independent brewers on legislative, regulatory, and industry-related matters. We discuss the impact of collective advocacy.

Craft Brewer Programs: Educational Resources

Craft beer associations offer educational programs and resources to help brewers navigate challenges and grow their businesses while preserving independence.

Conclusion

The challenges of staying independent in the craft beer industry are complex and multifaceted. Craft brewers face the allure of acquisition offers, the complexities of balancing growth with authenticity, and the ongoing battle for distribution and shelf space. As we continue our exploration of independent craft brewers and their fight for authenticity in the following chapters, we will delve deeper into the stories and experiences of specific breweries that have successfully navigated these challenges. Craft beer is not only a beverage; it is a testament to the dedication, creativity, and independence of its brewers, and the challenges they face are integral to the ongoing story of craft beer's authenticity.

Authenticity in Craft Brewing

Authenticity lies at the heart of the craft brewing ethos, encompassing a commitment to quality, tradition, innovation, and community. In this chapter, we explore the multifaceted concept of authenticity within the craft brewing industry, examining the ways in which craft brewers uphold and embody this vital principle.

Quality Craftsmanship: The Foundation of Authenticity

Craft brewers take immense pride in the quality and craftsmanship of their beers. We delve into the meticulous brewing processes and practices that underpin the authenticity of craft beer.

Small Batches, Big Impact

Craft brewers often produce beer in small batches to maintain quality control. We discuss how this approach allows for hands-on brewing and careful attention to detail.

Ingredient Sourcing: Local and Premium

Authentic craft brewers prioritize the sourcing of high-quality ingredients, often opting for locally grown or specialty ingredients to create distinctive flavors.

Brewing Tradition: Honoring the Past

Craft brewers draw inspiration from brewing traditions that have been passed down through generations. We explore how these traditions infuse authenticity into their beers.

Creativity and Innovation: Pushing Boundaries

Innovation is a hallmark of the craft beer movement. We discuss how craft brewers push the boundaries of flavor and technique, continually striving for unique and exciting brews.

Experimental Brewing: Bold Flavors

Craft brewers experiment with ingredients, styles, and techniques, resulting in a diverse range of beers that challenge conventional norms.

Collaborative Brewing: The Spirit of Craft

Collaborations between craft brewers, often known as "collab" beers, exemplify the spirit of innovation and camaraderie within the industry.

Community Engagement: Local Roots, Global Impact

Craft breweries often foster strong connections with their local communities. We explore how community engagement adds to the authenticity of craft beer.

Taproom Culture: A Sense of Belonging

Craft brewery taprooms serve as gathering places where locals and visitors alike can connect and enjoy beer together.

Support for Local Causes: Giving Back

Many craft breweries engage in charitable endeavors and support local causes, reinforcing their commitment to community.

Sustainability and Responsibility: Brewing for the Future

Sustainability practices are integral to the authenticity of craft brewing. We examine how craft brewers prioritize environmental responsibility.

Eco-Friendly Brewing: Reducing Footprints

Craft brewers implement eco-friendly practices such as energy efficiency, waste reduction, and water conservation.

Sourcing Responsibly: Supporting Local

Craft brewers often collaborate with local farmers and suppliers, contributing to local economies and reducing transportation-related environmental impacts.

Independence as a Pillar of Authenticity

Independence is a defining characteristic of craft brewers. We explore how ownership by small, traditional brewers underscores the authenticity of craft beer.

Defining Independence: Ownership Matters

Independence signifies ownership by those who are deeply passionate about the craft of brewing. We discuss why this pillar is integral to authenticity.

Resistance to Buyouts: Preserving Values

Many craft brewers resist acquisition offers from large beer corporations to maintain their independence and uphold their commitment to craft brewing.

The Art and Craft of Storytelling

Craft brewers often have compelling stories that resonate with consumers. We examine how storytelling contributes to the authenticity of craft beer.

Brewery Origins: Founding Stories

The stories of how breweries were founded, often rooted in passion and perseverance, connect consumers to the authentic spirit of craft beer.

Label Art and Design: Visual Narratives

Craft beer labels often feature unique artwork and designs that convey the brewery's personality and values.

Conclusion

Authenticity is the bedrock upon which the craft brewing industry is built. From quality craftsmanship to innovation, community engagement, sustainability, and the unwavering commitment to independence, craft brewers embody and celebrate authenticity in every pint they produce. As we continue our exploration of independent craft brewers and their fight for authenticity in the following chapters, we will delve deeper into the stories and experiences of specific breweries that exemplify the diverse facets of craft beer's authenticity. Craft beer is more than just a beverage; it is a reflection of the dedication, creativity, and integrity of its brewers, and these qualities will continue to shape its future.

Chapter 5: The Craft Beer Boom and Its Impact on the Beer Industry

The Growth of the Craft Beer Segment

The craft beer segment has experienced remarkable growth over the past few decades, reshaping the beer industry landscape. In this chapter, we explore the factors that have contributed to the explosive expansion of craft beer, examining the trends, consumer preferences, and economic impacts that have made it a dominant force in the beer world.

Early Days of Craft Beer

To understand the growth of the craft beer segment, we must first examine its humble beginnings. We delve into the early days of craft beer, tracing its roots back to a handful of pioneering breweries.

Birth of Microbreweries: A Brewing Revolution

Microbreweries, often seen as the precursors to modern craft breweries, initiated the craft beer movement in the 1970s and 1980s. We discuss how these small breweries sparked a revolution in brewing.

Pioneering Brewers: Visionaries of Flavor

Key figures in the early craft beer movement, such as Fritz Maytag of Anchor Brewing and Jack McAuliffe of New Albion Brewing, played pivotal roles in shaping the future of craft beer.

The Craft Beer Renaissance

The craft beer renaissance, marked by a resurgence of interest in traditional brewing techniques and diverse beer styles, breathed new life into the industry. We explore the factors that fueled this renaissance.

Consumer Desire for Flavor: A Paradigm Shift

Craft beer offered consumers a wide range of flavors and styles, challenging the dominance of mass-produced, light lagers. We discuss how this shift in consumer preferences drove the renaissance.

Brewing Creativity: Exploring Possibilities

Craft brewers embraced innovation and experimentation, creating unique and exciting beers that captivated beer enthusiasts. We examine the creative spirit that defined this era.

Explosive Brewery Growth

One of the defining features of the craft beer boom has been the sheer number of breweries that have opened their doors. We analyze the exponential growth of craft breweries and its impact.

Brewery Numbers: A Meteoric Rise

The craft beer segment has witnessed a rapid increase in the number of breweries, with thousands operating across the United States alone. We discuss the implications of this growth.

Local Brewery Movement: A Sense of Place

The rise of local breweries has created a sense of place and community, fostering connections between brewers and consumers. We explore the significance of localism in craft beer.

Beer Styles and Diversity

Craft beer is celebrated for its diversity of styles and flavors. We delve into the rich tapestry of beer styles that have emerged, from traditional ales and lagers to innovative hybrids.

Style Evolution: From Tradition to Experimentation

Craft brewers have reimagined classic styles and introduced innovative hybrids, creating a dynamic beer landscape. We explore some of the key beer styles that define craft brewing.

Regional Specialties: Local Flavors

Many craft breweries have embraced regional ingredients and traditions, leading to the development of unique beer specialties. We highlight examples of regional craft beer styles.

Economic Impact: Jobs and Revenue

The craft beer industry has not only transformed the beer landscape but also had a significant economic impact. We examine the contributions of craft beer to job creation and revenue generation.

Job Growth: Employment Opportunities

Craft breweries have become major employers in their communities, offering jobs in brewing, distribution, hospitality, and more.

Economic Contribution: Revenue and Tourism

Craft beer has injected billions of dollars into local and national economies, including revenue from brewery visits and beer tourism.

Market Share and Competition

Craft beer's growth has disrupted the beer industry hierarchy, challenging the dominance of multinational conglomerates. We discuss how craft breweries have gained market share and impacted the competitive landscape.

Market Share Trends: Craft vs. Macro

Craft beer has steadily gained market share, posing competition to large beer corporations. We explore the market dynamics and the changing beer landscape.

Conclusion

The craft beer segment's remarkable growth has been driven by a combination of factors, including consumer demand for flavor, brewing innovation, localism, economic contributions, and a dynamic diversity of beer styles. As we continue our exploration of the craft beer boom and its impact on the beer industry in the following chapters, we will delve deeper into the stories and experiences of specific breweries that have thrived during this era. Craft beer's ascent is not just a trend; it represents a fundamental shift in the way people perceive and enjoy beer, and its influence will continue to shape the industry's future.

Craft Beer's Influence on Consumer Preferences

The craft beer movement has had a profound influence on consumer preferences, reshaping the way people think about and enjoy beer. In this chapter, we explore how craft beer has redefined what consumers expect from their beer, examining the key factors that have driven this shift in preferences.

The Quest for Flavor and Variety

One of the most significant ways craft beer has influenced consumer preferences is by rekindling a passion for flavor and variety in beer. We delve into how craft beer has transformed consumers' expectations.

Flavor Exploration: Beyond Mass-Produced Lagers

Craft beer introduced consumers to a world of diverse flavors, encouraging them to explore a wide range of beer styles and taste profiles.

Pioneering Brews: Bold and Innovative

Craft brewers have pushed the boundaries of beer flavor by creating innovative and daring brews. We discuss how these pioneering beers have broadened consumers' horizons.

A Demand for Quality and Craftsmanship

Craft beer enthusiasts often prioritize quality and craftsmanship in their beer choices. We explore how the craft beer movement has elevated the standards for beer production.

Small Batch Production: Quality Control

Craft brewers' focus on small batch production allows for meticulous quality control, resulting in beers of consistently high quality.

Artisanal Brewing: Craftsmanship Matters

Consumers have come to appreciate the artisanal nature of craft brewing, valuing the hands-on approach and attention to detail that go into each batch.

The Shift from Brand Loyalty to Exploration

Unlike the traditional beer landscape, craft beer encourages consumers to explore a wide array of breweries and brands. We discuss how craft beer has shifted consumer loyalty from brands to experiences.

Brewery Visits: A New Beer Destination

Craft brewery taprooms have become destinations for beer enthusiasts, fostering a sense of community and connection to the brewing process.

Rotating Taps and Seasonals: Embracing Variety

Craft beer establishments often rotate their beer selections, encouraging consumers to try new styles and flavors. Seasonal releases add excitement to the craft beer experience.

Localism and Community Engagement

Craft breweries' strong ties to local communities have resonated with consumers who value supporting local businesses. We explore how localism has become a significant factor in consumer preferences.

Supporting Local: Economic Impact

Consumers understand that supporting local craft breweries contributes to local economies and job creation, making it a compelling choice.

Community Engagement: Beyond Beer

Craft breweries often engage with their communities through events, partnerships, and charitable endeavors. This community-focused approach resonates with consumers who seek a deeper connection to their beer.

Beer and Food Pairing

Craft beer has played a pivotal role in popularizing beer and food pairing as a culinary experience. We discuss how the craft beer movement has elevated the dining experience.

Beer Dinners: Culinary Adventures

Craft breweries and restaurants collaborate on beer dinners, where carefully crafted beer pairings enhance the dining experience.

Flavor Exploration: A Culinary Adventure

Consumers have embraced the idea that beer can be as versatile and complex as wine when it comes to pairing with food, leading to a surge in beer-related culinary exploration.

The Influence of Online Communities

Online communities and social media have played a significant role in shaping consumer preferences for craft beer. We explore how digital platforms have empowered beer enthusiasts.

Beer Rating Platforms: Crowd-Sourced Opinions

Websites and apps that allow users to rate and review beers have empowered consumers to make informed choices and share their beer experiences.

Social Media and Beer Influencers: Shaping Trends

Social media platforms and beer influencers have amplified the reach and impact of craft beer, helping to popularize specific styles, breweries, and trends.

Conclusion

Craft beer's influence on consumer preferences has been transformative, reinvigorating the beer industry and reshaping the way people engage with beer. As we continue our exploration of the craft beer boom and its impact on the beer industry in the following chapters, we will delve deeper into the stories and experiences of specific breweries and consumers who have been at the forefront of this revolution. Craft beer has not only rekindled a passion for beer but also ignited a desire for exploration, quality, and community, and these preferences will continue to define the beer landscape for years to come.

Big Beer's Response to the Craft Beer Boom

The craft beer movement has disrupted the traditional beer industry, prompting established giants, often referred to as "Big Beer," to respond to the growing popularity of craft beer. In this chapter, we explore how major beer corporations have reacted to the craft beer boom and the strategies they have employed to remain competitive in this evolving landscape.

Recognizing the Threat

The rapid rise of craft beer did not go unnoticed by Big Beer. We delve into how major beer corporations first perceived craft breweries as a potential threat to their market dominance.

Market Share Erosion: A Wake-Up Call

As craft beer's market share grew, Big Beer faced the reality of declining sales for their flagship brands, sparking concerns within the industry.

Acquisitions as a Defensive Strategy

Some major beer corporations began acquiring craft breweries to counter the threat and gain a foothold in the craft beer segment. We examine the motivations behind these acquisitions.

The Acquisition Trend

Acquisitions of craft breweries by Big Beer conglomerates became a defining feature of the industry's response to the craft beer boom. We explore notable acquisitions and their implications.

The Rise of "Crafty" Brands

Big Beer introduced brands designed to mimic the aesthetics and ethos of craft beer, blurring the lines between independent craft and mass-produced beer.

Controversies and Backlash

The acquisition trend generated controversies within the craft beer community, with some consumers feeling betrayed by breweries they had once considered independent.

Innovations and Craft-Style Brews

To compete with craft breweries, Big Beer began to innovate and introduce craft-style brews under their existing portfolios. We discuss the emergence of these "crafty" offerings.

Specialty and Seasonal Releases

Big Beer companies began producing specialty and seasonal beers designed to appeal to craft beer enthusiasts.

Embracing Variety: Exploring New Styles

Major beer corporations experimented with new beer styles, moving beyond their traditional lagers to meet evolving consumer preferences.

Distribution and Shelf Space Battles

Big Beer has leveraged its extensive distribution networks and financial resources to maintain a competitive edge in securing shelf space and distribution. We examine these competitive dynamics.

Shelf Space Dominance

Big Beer often commands significant shelf space in retail stores, making it challenging for craft breweries to compete for visibility.

Distribution Agreements: Contracts and Control

Major beer corporations have used distribution agreements to maintain control over the distribution of their products, further cementing their presence in the market.

Advertising and Marketing Strategies

Big Beer has invested heavily in advertising and marketing campaigns to maintain brand visibility and reach consumers. We explore the strategies employed.

Super Bowl Ads and Sponsorships

Big Beer companies have used high-profile events like the Super Bowl to showcase their brands and reach a broad audience.

Craft Beer Associations: Response to Big Beer Campaigns

Craft beer associations have countered Big Beer advertising campaigns by promoting the values of independent craft brewing.

Craft Beer Collaborations

Some Big Beer conglomerates have ventured into collaborations with craft breweries, blurring the lines between the two segments. We discuss the motivations and outcomes of these collaborations.

Exploring Collaboration Beers

Collaboration beers between craft breweries and Big Beer subsidiaries have generated mixed reactions within the craft beer community.

Impact on Craft Beer Identity

The response of Big Beer to the craft beer boom has raised questions about the integrity and identity of the craft beer movement. We explore how these dynamics have shaped perceptions of authenticity.

Independence and Authenticity Debates

The debate over what constitutes "craft" beer has intensified as more craft breweries become affiliated with major beer corporations.

Educating Consumers: Transparency and Definitions

Craft beer associations and independent craft brewers have sought to educate consumers about the importance of transparency and authenticity in beer.

Conclusion

Big Beer's response to the craft beer boom has been marked by acquisitions, innovation, distribution dominance, advertising campaigns, and collaborations. As we continue our exploration of the craft beer boom and its impact on the beer industry in the following chapters, we will delve deeper into the stories and experiences of craft breweries that have navigated these challenges and maintained their commitment to independence and authenticity. The response of Big Beer has shaped the craft beer landscape and ignited discussions about what it means to be a craft brewery in an evolving industry.

The Impact on Global Beer Trends

The craft beer boom has had a far-reaching impact on global beer trends, transcending borders and influencing brewing cultures worldwide. In this chapter, we explore how the rise of craft beer has reshaped the global beer industry, inspiring new brewing practices, consumer preferences, and innovations across the globe.

Exporting the Craft Beer Culture

Craft breweries in the United States, where the craft beer movement originated, have played a pivotal role in exporting the craft beer culture to other countries. We examine how American craft brewers have inspired breweries around the world.

Craft Beer Exports: Sharing Craft Excellence

American craft beer exports have introduced international consumers to a wide range of beer styles and flavors, fostering a global appreciation for craft beer.

Craft Beer Education: Training Brewmasters Abroad

American craft breweries have provided training and education opportunities for international brewmasters, contributing to the growth of craft beer knowledge and skills globally.

The Rise of Craft Beer in Europe

Europe, with its rich brewing traditions, has experienced a resurgence of interest in craft beer. We explore how craft beer has revitalized European brewing scenes.

Craft Beer in Beer-Steeped Europe

Historically, Europe was known for its traditional beer styles, but craft breweries have introduced innovation and variety, reshaping beer culture on the continent.

Microbreweries and Nanobreweries: A European Renaissance

Microbreweries and nanobreweries have proliferated in Europe, challenging the dominance of established brewing giants and reviving small-scale, artisanal brewing.

Craft Beer in Asia: A Growing Phenomenon

Asia has witnessed a burgeoning craft beer movement. We discuss how craft beer has gained popularity and recognition in countries like Japan, South Korea, and China.

Emerging Craft Beer Scenes

Countries in Asia have seen the emergence of vibrant craft beer scenes, with local breweries producing unique and culturally inspired brews.

Craft Beer and Culinary Fusion

In Asia, craft beer has become an integral part of culinary experimentation, with breweries collaborating with restaurants to create fusion dishes and pairings.

Latin America: Craft Beer on the Rise

Latin America has embraced the craft beer movement, with breweries in countries like Mexico and Brazil garnering attention for their innovative brews. We explore the craft beer scene in the region.

Mexican Craft Beer: Beyond Cerveza

Mexico has emerged as a significant player in the craft beer world, challenging stereotypes of Mexican beer with a diverse range of styles.

Brazil's Craft Beer Revolution

Craft beer has experienced rapid growth in Brazil, with breweries offering tropical and innovative flavors that resonate with local tastes.

Craft Beer in Africa: An Emerging Trend

Craft beer has started to make its mark in Africa, offering a contrast to the dominance of mass-produced lagers. We discuss the challenges and opportunities faced by African craft brewers.

South African Craft Beer Scene

South Africa has seen a surge in craft breweries, with a focus on unique ingredients and local flavors.

Craft Beer and Entrepreneurship in Africa

Craft breweries in Africa often combine entrepreneurship with a passion for brewing, contributing to economic development and job creation.

International Collaborations and Experiments

Craft breweries worldwide have embraced international collaborations and experimental brews, leading to a cross-pollination of beer styles and techniques. We explore the creative exchanges that have taken place.

Collaborative Brews: Global Partnerships

Craft brewers from different countries have collaborated on special beers, resulting in exciting blends of traditions and flavors.

Importing Global Ingredients: Unique Brews

Breweries have been importing ingredients from various corners of the world to create distinctive, internationally inspired brews.

Craft Beer in an Evolving Industry

The global influence of craft beer has disrupted traditional beer markets and pushed larger beer corporations to adapt and innovate. We discuss how craft beer has catalyzed change in the global beer industry.

Big Beer's Response Worldwide

Major beer corporations around the world have responded to the craft beer movement by acquiring craft breweries and introducing craft-style brews.

Craft Beer Events and Tourism

Craft beer has given rise to international beer festivals and beer tourism, providing opportunities for beer enthusiasts to explore new flavors and cultures.

Conclusion

The craft beer boom has transcended borders, inspiring a global renaissance in brewing that spans North America, Europe, Asia, Latin America, and Africa. As we continue our exploration of the craft beer boom and its impact on the beer industry in the following chapters, we will delve deeper into the stories and experiences of specific breweries and individuals who have played pivotal roles in shaping the global craft beer movement. Craft beer is no longer confined to a single region; it has become a symbol of innovation, diversity, and creativity that resonates with beer lovers worldwide, leaving an indelible mark on the global beer landscape.

Chapter 6: The Art and Science of Craft Brewing

Mastering the Craft of Brewing

Craft brewing is a delicate balance of art and science, where brewers combine creativity with precise techniques to produce unique and exceptional beers. In this chapter, we delve into the intricate world of mastering the craft of brewing, exploring the key elements that contribute to brewing excellence.

The Brewer's Palette: Ingredients and Flavor

At the heart of craft brewing is the artistry of flavor creation through the careful selection and manipulation of ingredients.

Malt Mastery: The Foundation of Flavor

Malt is the canvas upon which brewers paint their flavors. We delve into the role of malt in brewing and how different malts contribute to various beer styles.

Hop Alchemy: Bittering, Aroma, and Beyond

Hops are the spice of beer, providing bitterness, aroma, and a range of flavors. We explore the art of hop selection and addition.

Yeast Magic: Fermentation and Flavor Transformation

Yeast is the brewer's magical agent, converting sugars into alcohol and generating a myriad of flavors. We discuss yeast strains, fermentation temperatures, and their impact on beer profiles.

Brewing Techniques: From Mash to Boil

The brewing process involves a series of carefully timed and temperature-controlled steps, each influencing the final beer.

Mashing In: Extracting Sugars and Flavors

Mashing is the first critical step where grains meet hot water to extract sugars and flavors. We detail the mashing process and its significance.

The Boil: Flavor Extraction and Sanitization

The boil not only extracts hop bitterness but also serves as a sanitization step. We discuss the boil's role in shaping beer.

Cooling and Fermentation: Managing Temperatures

Cooling the wort and controlling fermentation temperatures are crucial for achieving desired flavor profiles and yeast activity. We explore the importance of temperature control.

Water Chemistry: The Hidden Ingredient

Water quality and composition have a significant impact on beer flavor. We delve into water chemistry and how brewers adjust their water profiles.

pH Levels: Balancing Act

Maintaining the right pH level in the brewing process is essential for enzyme activity and yeast health.

Brewing Salts: Adjusting Water Chemistry

Brewers use salts like gypsum and calcium chloride to modify water profiles and enhance flavors.

Quality Control: Sensory Evaluation

Craft brewers employ rigorous quality control measures, including sensory evaluation, to ensure consistent beer excellence.

Sensory Panels: Training Palates

Sensory panels comprised of trained tasters assess beer attributes like aroma, flavor, mouthfeel, and appearance. We discuss the importance of sensory evaluation.

Off-Flavors: Identifying and Correcting

Brewers must be adept at identifying off-flavors and their causes to maintain beer quality.

Creative Recipe Development

Craft brewers constantly experiment with ingredients and techniques to craft new and innovative beers.

Homebrew Roots: Scaling Up Ideas

Many craft brewers start as homebrewers, refining their skills and experimenting with new recipes before going commercial.

Seasonal Brews and Limited Releases: Innovation in Action

Craft breweries often release seasonal and limited-edition beers to showcase creativity and keep their offerings fresh.

Sustainability and Efficiency

Sustainability practices are integral to craft brewing, both from an environmental and economic standpoint.

Waste Reduction: Repurposing Byproducts

Breweries find creative ways to reduce waste, repurposing spent grains, hops, and yeast for other purposes.

Energy Efficiency: Green Brewing

Craft breweries explore energy-efficient processes and renewable energy sources to reduce their environmental footprint.

The Quest for Consistency

Maintaining consistent quality is a challenge for craft brewers as they scale up production. We discuss the strategies brewers use to ensure consistency.

Recipe Scaling: Precise Calculations

Scaling up recipes from small to large batches requires precise calculations to maintain the intended flavor profile.

Quality Assurance Programs: Documentation and Control

Craft breweries implement quality assurance programs to monitor and control all aspects of production.

Conclusion

Mastering the craft of brewing is a dynamic and ever-evolving journey for craft brewers. Through the careful selection of ingredients, precise brewing techniques, quality control measures, creative recipe development, and a commitment to sustainability, craft brewers continue to push the boundaries of beer excellence. In the following chapters, we will explore the role of ingredients in craft beer, the creative process of craft beer development, and the spirit of innovation and experimentation that drives the craft brewing industry forward. The craft of brewing is a blend of tradition, innovation, and artistry that results in the diverse and extraordinary beers enjoyed by enthusiasts worldwide.

The Role of Ingredients in Craft Beer

Craft brewing is a craft that relies heavily on the selection and manipulation of ingredients to create unique and memorable beer experiences. In this chapter, we explore the fundamental role that ingredients play in the craft beer-making process, from the choice of grains and hops to yeast strains and additional flavorings.

Grains: The Foundation of Beer

Grains provide the essential sugars needed for fermentation and contribute a significant portion of a beer's flavor and character.

Malt Varieties: A World of Flavor

We delve into the diverse range of malt varieties used in craft brewing and how they impact the color, aroma, and taste of beer.

Specialty Grains: Adding Complexity

Craft brewers often incorporate specialty grains like roasted barley, oats, and wheat to add complexity and unique characteristics to their beers.

Hops: The Spice of Beer

Hops are responsible for the bitterness, aroma, and flavor of beer, making them a vital ingredient in crafting distinctive beer profiles.

Hop Varieties: Aromatics and Bitterness

We explore the vast array of hop varieties available to craft brewers, each contributing unique aromatics and bitterness levels.

Hop Additions: Timing and Techniques

Craft brewers carefully consider when and how to add hops during the brewing process, affecting both bitterness and aroma.

Yeast: The Magical Microorganism

Yeast is the workhorse of fermentation, converting sugars into alcohol and producing a wide range of flavors and aromas.

Yeast Strains: Diversity and Expression

Different yeast strains offer varied flavor profiles, and craft brewers select strains to achieve specific beer styles and characteristics.

Fermentation Temperatures: Controlling Flavor

Fermentation temperature plays a crucial role in determining the flavor compounds produced by yeast, influencing the final beer's taste.

Water: The Unsung Hero

Water may seem mundane, but its quality and mineral composition significantly affect the flavor and mouthfeel of beer.

Water Profiles: Building the Foundation

We discuss how craft brewers adjust water profiles to match beer styles, highlighting the role of minerals like calcium, sulfate, and chloride.

Water Sources: Local Terroir

Craft brewers often use local water sources, embracing the unique characteristics of their region's water in their beer.

Additional Flavorings: Creativity Unleashed

Craft brewers frequently experiment with additional flavorings to create unique and innovative beer experiences.

Fruits, Spices, and More: Creative Additions

We explore the use of fruits, spices, herbs, and other flavorings in craft beer, showcasing breweries that push the boundaries of traditional ingredients.

Barrel Aging: Maturation and Complexity

Craft brewers utilize various types of barrels, such as bourbon and wine barrels, to impart additional flavors and complexity to their beers.

Collaborations and Local Sourcing

Craft brewers often collaborate with local farmers and producers to source ingredients, fostering a sense of community and sustainability.

Farm-to-Table Brewing: Local Partnerships

We highlight craft breweries that work closely with local farms to source grains, hops, and other ingredients.

Ingredient Transparency: A Connection with Consumers

Craft breweries often emphasize ingredient transparency, allowing consumers to trace the origins of the ingredients used in their beer.

Sustainability and Ingredient Sourcing

Sustainability practices extend to ingredient sourcing, with craft brewers seeking environmentally responsible options.

Organic and Locally Sourced Ingredients

We explore how some craft breweries prioritize organic and locally sourced ingredients to minimize their environmental impact.

Waste Reduction: Repurposing Ingredients

Craft brewers find innovative ways to reduce waste by repurposing spent grains, hops, and other byproducts.

The Art of Recipe Development

The art of crafting a beer recipe is where creativity, tradition, and science converge to produce unique and memorable brews.

Homebrew Roots: Small-Scale Innovation

Many craft brewers start as homebrewers, experimenting with recipes in small batches before scaling up.

Seasonal and Limited Releases: A Showcase of Creativity

Craft breweries often release seasonal and limited-edition beers that highlight their creativity and innovation.

Conclusion

Ingredients are the building blocks of craft beer, and their careful selection, combination, and manipulation are central to the craft brewer's art. In the following chapters, we will explore the creative process of craft beer development, the role of innovation and experimentation, and the pursuit of excellence that drives the craft brewing industry. Craft brewers continue to push the boundaries of what is possible in brewing, using ingredients as their palette to create exceptional and diverse beer experiences for enthusiasts around the world.

The Creative Process of Craft Beer Development

Craft brewing is a dynamic and creative process that goes beyond simply following a recipe. In this chapter, we delve into the intricate and innovative creative process that craft brewers undertake to develop unique and memorable beers. From concept to execution, we explore how craft brewers push the boundaries, experiment with new ideas, and craft exceptional brews that captivate beer enthusiasts.

Inspiration: The Birth of an Idea

Craft beer development often begins with a spark of inspiration, a concept, or a desire to explore new flavors and styles.

Historical and Cultural Influences

We discuss how history, culture, and traditions can inspire craft brewers to revisit classic beer styles or create entirely new ones.

Ingredient Exploration

The selection of unique and locally sourced ingredients can serve as a starting point for creative experimentation.

Recipe Design: Balancing Art and Science

The craft of designing a beer recipe involves a delicate balance of artistry and scientific precision.

The Malt Bill: Building the Foundation

We explore how craft brewers select and combine various malt varieties to create the desired color, flavor, and body in their beer.

Hop Selection: Aromatics and Bitterness

Craft brewers carefully choose hop varieties and plan their additions to achieve specific aroma and flavor profiles while controlling bitterness.

Yeast Strain Considerations

The choice of yeast strain can dramatically impact the beer's character, and craft brewers select strains that align with their vision.

Experimentation and Innovation

Craft brewers are known for their willingness to experiment and innovate, pushing the boundaries of traditional beer styles.

Pilot Batches: Small-Scale Creativity

Many craft breweries conduct pilot batches to test new recipes and ideas on a small scale before committing to a full production run.

Collaborations: Creative Partnerships

Collaborations between breweries, chefs, and other artisans bring fresh perspectives and creative ingredients into the brewing process.

Brewing Techniques: Shaping Flavor

The craft of brewing involves a range of techniques to achieve specific flavor profiles and characteristics.

Temperature Control: Precision in Fermentation

Craft brewers meticulously control fermentation temperatures to extract desired flavors and esters from yeast.

Barrel Aging: Maturation and Complexity

We explore the art of barrel aging, which imparts additional flavors, aromas, and complexity to beer.

Quality Control: Refining the Craft

Maintaining consistent quality is paramount for craft brewers, and quality control processes are integrated into the creative process.

Sensory Evaluation: Tasting the Vision

Sensory panels assess the beer throughout the development process to ensure it aligns with the intended flavor profile.

Adjustments and Iterations

Craft brewers are open to making adjustments and iterations as they refine their recipes, ensuring the final product meets their creative vision.

Label Design and Branding

The creative process extends beyond brewing to label design and branding, where storytelling plays a crucial role in connecting with consumers.

Label Artistry: Visual Appeal

We explore how craft breweries collaborate with artists to create visually striking labels that reflect the beer's identity.

Storytelling: Connecting with Consumers

Craft brewers often craft compelling narratives about their beer's origin, ingredients, and inspiration to engage consumers on a deeper level.

Launch and Presentation

Craft brewers carefully plan the launch and presentation of their beers to create a memorable experience for consumers.

Release Events: Building Anticipation

Craft breweries often host release events and tastings to generate excitement and create a sense of community.

Glassware and Serving: Enhancing the Experience

The choice of glassware and serving techniques can enhance the beer-drinking experience and highlight its unique qualities.

Consumer Feedback and Adaptation

Craft brewers value consumer feedback and use it to adapt and refine their beers, fostering a sense of community and collaboration.

Engaging with Enthusiasts

Craft breweries often engage with beer enthusiasts to gather feedback, hosting events and social media interactions.

Seasonal and Limited Releases

Craft brewers often release seasonal and limited-edition beers based on consumer demand and feedback.

Conclusion

The creative process of craft beer development is a dynamic and multifaceted journey that begins with inspiration and culminates in the presentation of a unique and exceptional beer. In the following chapters, we will explore the spirit of innovation and experimentation that drives the craft brewing industry, delving deeper into the stories of specific breweries and individuals who have pushed the boundaries of brewing creativity. The craft of brewing is a fusion of tradition, innovation, and artistic expression that continues to captivate and inspire beer enthusiasts worldwide.

Brewing Innovation and Experimentation

Innovation and experimentation are the lifeblood of the craft brewing industry, driving the creation of new styles, flavors, and brewing techniques. In this chapter, we explore how craft brewers continually push the boundaries of what's possible in brewing, embracing creativity and exploration to craft exceptional and groundbreaking beers.

Brewing Beyond Tradition

Craft brewers are renowned for their willingness to challenge traditional brewing norms and venture into uncharted territories.

Reviving Forgotten Styles

We explore how craft brewers have revived obscure or forgotten beer styles, bringing them back into the spotlight.

Hybrid Styles: Blending Traditions

Brewers often experiment with blending different beer styles to create hybrid brews that defy categorization.

Unique Ingredients and Flavorings

The quest for innovation often involves incorporating unconventional and unique ingredients into the brewing process.

Experimental Hops and Grains

Craft brewers frequently experiment with new hop and grain varieties to introduce novel flavors and aromas.

Unusual Additions: Spices, Fruits, and More

We delve into how craft brewers use spices, fruits, herbs, and other unconventional ingredients to create one-of-a-kind brews.

Barrel Aging and Mixed Fermentation

Craft brewers have pioneered barrel aging and mixed fermentation techniques, leading to a new realm of complexity and flavor.

Barrel Aging: Beyond Oak

We explore the diverse range of barrels, including wine, whiskey, and even tequila barrels, used for aging beer.

Wild and Sour Ales

Craft brewers have embraced wild yeast strains and mixed fermentation processes to produce sour and complex ales.

Collaborations: A Collective Creative Spirit

Collaborations between breweries, often with different specialties and perspectives, have resulted in some of the most innovative and exciting beers.

Creative Partnerships

We discuss the art of collaboration between breweries, chefs, coffee roasters, and other artisans to create unique brews.

Collaboration Festivals

Craft beer festivals dedicated to collaborations provide a platform for brewers to showcase their innovative creations.

Experimental Techniques: Pushing the Limits

Craft brewers continually explore experimental brewing techniques that challenge conventional practices.

Dry Hopping: Variations and Beyond

We delve into the art of dry hopping, including double, triple, and even quadruple dry hopping techniques.

Extreme Brewing: High ABV and Beyond

Craft brewers experiment with extreme beer styles, including high-alcohol brews, spiced beers, and dessert-inspired creations.

Sustainability and Innovation

Innovation extends to sustainable brewing practices, as craft brewers seek eco-friendly solutions.

Closed-Loop Systems

We explore how some craft breweries have implemented closed-loop systems to minimize waste and energy usage.

Alternative Ingredients: Redefining Tradition

Craft brewers experiment with alternative ingredients like alternative grains (e.g., quinoa, millet) and edible flowers to reduce environmental impact.

Small-Batch and Limited Releases

Craft brewers often use small-batch and limited-release beers as a canvas for innovation and experimentation.

Small-Batch Series

We discuss how some craft breweries have dedicated series to experimental and limited-edition brews.

Consumer Feedback and Adaptation

Craft breweries value consumer feedback on experimental releases and use it to adapt and refine their brewing techniques.

Ethical and Sustainable Brewing

Innovation extends to ethical and sustainable brewing practices, as craft brewers prioritize environmental and social responsibility.

Social Initiatives

Some craft breweries support social causes and initiatives, using beer as a vehicle for positive change.

Sustainable Packaging: Reducing Environmental Impact

Craft breweries explore eco-friendly packaging options, such as recyclable cans and biodegradable materials.

Conclusion

Innovation and experimentation are at the heart of the craft brewing ethos, driving the industry forward and captivating the imaginations of beer enthusiasts worldwide. The passion for pushing the boundaries of brewing, embracing unique ingredients, and challenging traditional practices ensures that craft brewing remains a dynamic and ever-evolving craft. In the following chapters, we will continue to explore the stories of breweries and individuals who have made groundbreaking contributions to the world of craft beer, further illustrating the industry's spirit of innovation and exploration.

Chapter 7: Craft Beer Culture and Community
The Rise of Beer Enthusiasts and Connoisseurs

As craft beer has grown in popularity and diversity, so too has the community of beer enthusiasts and connoisseurs. In this chapter, we explore the evolution of beer appreciation, from casual sippers to passionate connoisseurs, and the pivotal role they play in shaping the craft beer culture.

The Birth of Beer Enthusiasts

Craft beer culture was propelled by the enthusiasm of early adopters who sought more from their beer-drinking experience.

The Homebrewing Connection

Many early craft beer enthusiasts were homebrewers who shared a deep curiosity about the brewing process and ingredients.

Exploring New Flavors

Craft beer offered a wide array of flavors and styles, encouraging enthusiasts to explore and savor the diverse world of beer.

The Rise of Beer Connoisseurs

Beer appreciation evolved into a refined art form as enthusiasts became connoisseurs, analyzing beer with sophistication and nuance.

Tasting and Evaluation

We explore the sensory evaluation techniques employed by beer connoisseurs, including aroma, flavor, mouthfeel, and appearance.

Beer Pairing: A Culinary Adventure

Connoisseurs appreciate the intricate dance of flavors when pairing beer with food, elevating the dining experience.

Beer Education and Certification

As beer knowledge became more specialized, formal education and certification programs emerged to recognize expertise.

Cicerone Certification: Beer Sommeliers

The Cicerone program trains and certifies individuals as beer experts, akin to sommeliers in the wine world.

Brewing and Sensory Analysis Courses

Beer enthusiasts can enroll in courses covering brewing techniques, ingredient analysis, and sensory evaluation to deepen their knowledge.

Beer Rating and Review Platforms

The digital age brought about the rise of online platforms where beer enthusiasts share their opinions, contributing to a global beer conversation.

RateBeer and Beer Advocate

We discuss how platforms like RateBeer and Beer Advocate provide spaces for enthusiasts to review and rate beers.

Untappd: Social Beer Sharing

Untappd combines beer ratings with social networking, allowing users to share their beer experiences with friends and the global community.

Beer Festivals and Events

Beer festivals have become a hub for enthusiasts to explore new beers, meet brewers, and celebrate the craft beer culture.

Craft Beer Festivals Worldwide

We explore some of the most renowned craft beer festivals globally, such as the Great American Beer Festival and the Great British Beer Festival.

Collaborative and Specialty Events

Craft breweries often collaborate on festival-exclusive beers, adding an element of excitement for attendees.

The Role of Beer Media

Beer enthusiasts and connoisseurs contribute to and consume a vast array of beer-related media.

Beer Blogs and Publications

We discuss how beer enthusiasts often share their experiences and reviews through blogs and magazines.

Beer Podcasts and YouTube Channels

The rise of digital media has led to an explosion of beer-related podcasts and YouTube channels, further connecting the community.

Beer Collecting and Cellaring

Some connoisseurs take their passion to the next level by collecting and aging beers, creating personal cellars.

Collectible Bottles and Labels

We explore the world of collectible beer bottles and labels, prized for their rarity and artwork.

Aging and Vertical Tastings

Connoisseurs age beers to allow flavors to develop and organize vertical tastings to compare different vintages.

Beer Tourism

Enthusiasts travel to breweries, beer destinations, and hop-growing regions to immerse themselves in the world of craft beer.

Brewery Visits and Tours

We discuss how brewery visits provide enthusiasts with insights into the brewing process and the opportunity to meet brewers.

Beer Trails and Destination Breweries

Craft beer tourism has spawned beer trails and destination breweries, boosting local economies.

Community Engagement and Giving Back

Beer enthusiasts often use their passion for beer as a means of giving back to their communities.

Charity Beer Events

We explore how beer enthusiasts organize charity events, where the proceeds benefit local causes.

Collaborative Brews for a Cause

Craft breweries collaborate with enthusiasts to brew special beers, with proceeds donated to charitable organizations.

Conclusion

The rise of beer enthusiasts and connoisseurs has transformed the world of craft beer, elevating the appreciation of beer to an art form. Their passion, knowledge, and dedication to the craft have enriched the beer culture and created a sense of community that transcends borders. In the following chapters, we will continue to explore the broader craft beer community, including the role of beer festivals, online communities, and the social aspect of craft beer, further highlighting the vibrant and dynamic culture that has emerged around this beloved beverage.

Beer Festivals and Events

Beer festivals and events have become central to the craft beer culture, providing enthusiasts with opportunities to explore new beers, meet brewers, and celebrate their shared passion. In this chapter, we delve into the world of beer festivals and events, exploring their history, diversity, and significance within the craft beer community.

The Origin of Beer Festivals

Beer festivals have a rich history dating back centuries, often rooted in local traditions and celebrations.

Oktoberfest: A Legendary Tradition

We explore the origins of Oktoberfest in Munich, Germany, and its transformation into the world's largest beer festival.

Early American Beer Festivals

In the United States, beer festivals gained popularity in the late 20th century, mirroring the growth of the craft beer movement.

The Diversity of Beer Festivals

Beer festivals come in a wide variety of forms, from small local gatherings to large international events.

Local and Regional Festivals

We discuss the charm of local and regional beer festivals, which often focus on showcasing nearby breweries.

International Beer Festivals

Some beer festivals draw enthusiasts from around the world, celebrating a global spectrum of beer styles.

Notable Beer Festivals Worldwide

Several beer festivals have gained renown for their size, unique themes, or the quality of beers they feature.

Great American Beer Festival (GABF)

We explore the history and significance of GABF, one of the largest and most prestigious beer festivals in the U.S.

Belgian Beer Weekend

Belgium's celebration of its beer heritage is a must-visit for enthusiasts seeking the world's finest Belgian brews.

The Great British Beer Festival (GBBF)

GBBF showcases the rich tradition of British brewing, featuring a vast array of real ales and cask-conditioned beers.

Collaborative and Specialty Events

Craft breweries often collaborate to create exclusive festival beers, adding excitement to these gatherings.

Collaboration Festivals

We delve into festivals where breweries collaborate on unique beers, showcasing the spirit of cooperation in the craft beer world.

Specialty and Themed Events

Craft beer festivals with specific themes, such as sour beer festivals or barrel-aged beer events, cater to enthusiasts with distinct tastes.

The Festival Experience

Beer festivals offer attendees a unique experience beyond just beer tasting, often incorporating entertainment and food.

Live Music and Entertainment

We discuss the role of live music, games, and other forms of entertainment in enhancing the festival atmosphere.

Food Pairings and Culinary Experiences

Many beer festivals include food vendors or pairings, demonstrating the synergy between beer and cuisine.

Meet the Brewer

One of the highlights of beer festivals is the opportunity to meet the brewers behind the beers.

Brewer Q&A Sessions

Enthusiasts can engage with brewers in Q&A sessions, gaining insights into their brewing philosophies and techniques.

Collaborative Brews

Festivals often feature collaborative brews where brewers come together to craft unique beers specifically for the event.

The Impact on Local Economies

Beer festivals provide a significant economic boost to the host cities and regions.

Tourism and Hospitality

We explore how beer tourism and hospitality industries benefit from the influx of festival attendees.

Supporting Local Businesses

Local businesses, including restaurants, hotels, and transportation services, see increased revenue during festival weekends.

Evolving Beer Festivals in the Digital Age

The digital age has transformed the way beer festivals are organized, promoted, and experienced.

Ticketing and Registration

Online ticketing platforms and mobile apps have streamlined the registration process for attendees.

Social Media and Beer Festivals

We discuss how social media has become a powerful tool for promoting beer festivals and connecting attendees.

Sustainability Initiatives

Many beer festivals prioritize sustainability, implementing eco-friendly practices to reduce their environmental impact.

Recycling and Waste Reduction

Festivals often incorporate recycling programs and waste reduction measures to minimize their carbon footprint.

Eco-Friendly Vendors

We explore how some festivals partner with eco-conscious vendors who prioritize sustainable practices.

Conclusion

Beer festivals and events are more than just opportunities to enjoy beer; they are celebrations of the craft, culture, and community that have grown around it. From traditional festivals with centuries-old traditions to modern, innovative events that push the boundaries of beer appreciation, these gatherings showcase the diverse and vibrant world of craft beer. In the following chapters, we will continue to explore the craft beer community, including the role of online communities, beer enthusiasts, and the social aspect of craft beer, providing a comprehensive view of this dynamic and evolving culture.

The Role of Online Communities

The craft beer community has expanded beyond local breweries and festivals, finding a virtual home in online communities. In this chapter, we explore the profound impact of online platforms, forums, and social media groups on the craft beer culture. These digital spaces have become hubs for enthusiasts to connect, share knowledge, and deepen their appreciation for the world of craft beer.

The Digital Revolution in Craft Beer

The advent of the internet and social media has transformed the way craft beer enthusiasts connect and engage with the industry.

Emergence of Online Beer Communities

We discuss the early days of online beer communities, highlighting their evolution and growth.

The Proliferation of Beer Blogs and Websites

Beer enthusiasts and experts alike have created blogs and websites to share reviews, news, and insights.

The Diversity of Online Beer Communities

Online beer communities take various forms, catering to enthusiasts with different interests and levels of expertise.

Beer Rating and Review Platforms

We delve into platforms like RateBeer, Beer Advocate, and Untappd, where enthusiasts rate and review beers and interact with others.

Social Media Groups

Beer-related groups on platforms like Facebook and Reddit provide spaces for enthusiasts to discuss and share their passion.

Specialty Forums and Homebrewing Communities

We explore the role of niche forums dedicated to specific beer styles, brewing techniques, and homebrewing.

Connecting with Beer Enthusiasts Worldwide

Online beer communities transcend geographical boundaries, fostering connections among enthusiasts globally.

Sharing Beer Experiences

Enthusiasts share their beer experiences, recommendations, and discoveries from around the world.

Virtual Tastings and Bottle Shares

We discuss how virtual tastings and bottle shares have become popular among online beer communities, allowing members to sample and discuss beers together.

Access to Beer Knowledge and Education

Online communities serve as valuable resources for expanding beer knowledge and expertise.

Beer Education and Certification

We explore how platforms like the Cicerone program and online courses provide accessible beer education.

Expert Q&A Sessions

Online beer communities often host Q&A sessions with industry professionals, allowing enthusiasts to learn from experts.

Beer Trading and Collecting

The digital age has facilitated beer trading and collecting, allowing enthusiasts to access rare and sought-after brews.

Beer Trading Platforms

We discuss the role of online platforms where enthusiasts can trade beers and build their collections.

Collecting and Cellaring Advice

Online communities provide guidance on beer collecting, cellaring, and aging techniques.

Building Local and Global Communities

Online beer communities foster a sense of belonging and provide a platform for local and global connections.

Regional Beer Groups

We explore how regional beer groups on social media connect enthusiasts within specific geographic areas.

International Beer Exchange

Enthusiasts from different countries often exchange beer packages and participate in international beer exchanges.

Influencer Culture in Craft Beer

Online influencers and content creators have played a significant role in shaping craft beer culture and trends.

Beer Reviewers and YouTubers

We discuss the rise of beer reviewers and YouTubers who share their tasting experiences and insights with a global audience.

Social Media Influencers

Social media influencers collaborate with breweries and share their beer journeys, influencing trends and consumer preferences.

Online Beer Controversies and Debates

Online beer communities are not without their share of controversies and debates, reflecting the diversity of opinions within the craft beer world.

Controversial Releases and Brewery Behavior

We explore instances where controversial beer releases and brewery actions have sparked heated discussions.

Debates on Beer Styles and Trends

Online communities engage in debates about the authenticity of beer styles, the influence of trends, and the role of tradition.

The Future of Online Beer Communities

Online beer communities continue to evolve, impacting the craft beer culture in new and dynamic ways.

Digital Beer Festivals and Events

We discuss the rise of virtual beer festivals and events in response to changing circumstances.

Beer Technology and Innovation

Online communities are at the forefront of discussing beer-related technology and innovation, such as beer apps and digital brewing.

Conclusion

Online beer communities have become indispensable in the world of craft beer, fostering connections, knowledge sharing, and a sense of belonging among enthusiasts. As the craft beer culture continues to evolve, online platforms will undoubtedly play an even greater role in shaping its future. In the following chapters, we will further explore the craft beer community, including the role of beer enthusiasts, the social aspect of craft beer, and the ongoing influence of craft beer on beer culture at large.

The Social Aspect of Craft Beer

Craft beer is not just a beverage; it's a social experience that brings people together. In this chapter, we explore the social dimension of craft beer, from the camaraderie among beer enthusiasts to the role of breweries as community hubs. The craft beer culture thrives on the connections and relationships that it fosters, creating a vibrant and inclusive community.

The Craft Beer Community: A Gathering of Enthusiasts

Craft beer enthusiasts form a diverse and passionate community that transcends boundaries and backgrounds.

Beer Enthusiast Gatherings

We discuss how beer enthusiasts organize and attend gatherings, tastings, and bottle shares to connect with like-minded individuals.

The Craft Beer Trade

Enthusiasts often engage in beer trading, exchanging rare and sought-after brews with fellow aficionados.

The Role of Breweries as Gathering Places

Craft breweries have become more than production facilities; they are community hubs and social spaces.

Taprooms and Brewpubs

We explore how taprooms and brewpubs provide environments for socializing, enjoying beer, and connecting with brewers.

Brewery Events and Activities

Breweries host a variety of events, from release parties and live music to trivia nights and yoga classes, fostering a sense of community.

The Significance of Beer Release Events

Craft beer release events generate excitement and anticipation within the community.

Limited Edition and Specialty Releases

We discuss how breweries create buzz around limited edition and specialty releases, often drawing long lines of eager enthusiasts.

Campouts and Overnight Events

Enthusiasts sometimes camp out overnight to secure coveted releases, turning these events into social gatherings.

Beer Festivals as Social Celebrations

Beer festivals are more than just opportunities to taste beer; they are vibrant celebrations of the craft.

Festivals as Reunions

Enthusiasts often use festivals as opportunities to reunite with friends and fellow enthusiasts from near and far.

Community and Collaboration Beers

Craft breweries collaborate on festival-exclusive beers, embodying the spirit of community and creativity.

Online Communities as Social Spaces

The digital age has transformed craft beer into a global and interconnected community.

Virtual Tastings and Meetups

Online communities organize virtual tastings and meetups, allowing members to share beers and stories regardless of geographic location.

Beer Trade and Sharing Platforms

Enthusiasts trade and share beers through online platforms, building connections and expanding their beer horizons.

The Role of Beer Enthusiast Clubs

Beer enthusiast clubs provide a structured way for individuals to share their passion and engage in social activities.

Homebrew Clubs

We discuss the role of homebrew clubs in bringing together aspiring and experienced brewers to share knowledge and brew together.

Tasting and Appreciation Clubs

Enthusiast clubs often organize tastings, appreciation events, and educational sessions, deepening members' beer knowledge.

The Social Impact of Craft Beer

Craft beer has the power to create meaningful connections and positive social change.

Community Engagement and Charity

Craft breweries frequently engage with their communities through charity events and partnerships, supporting local causes.

Beer and Food Pairing Dinners

We explore how beer and food pairing dinners offer unique culinary experiences and promote community.

The Inclusivity of Craft Beer

Craft beer strives to be inclusive and welcoming, breaking down barriers and stereotypes.

Diversity and Inclusion Initiatives

We discuss the efforts made by the craft beer industry to promote diversity, equity, and inclusion.

Beer as a Bridge

Beer has the ability to bring people from diverse backgrounds together, fostering understanding and friendship.

Conclusion

Craft beer is not just about what's in the glass; it's about the connections and relationships that form around it. From taprooms and festivals to online communities and charity events, craft beer creates a sense of belonging and camaraderie that transcends borders and backgrounds. As the craft beer culture continues to evolve, its social aspect will remain at its core, bringing people together in the name of great beer and great company. In the following chapters, we will further explore the craft beer community, including the impact of craft beer on beer culture at large and the ongoing evolution of this dynamic and inclusive culture.

Conclusion
Celebrating the Craft Beer Renaissance

As we reach the culmination of our journey through the world of craft beer, it is clear that we are in the midst of a Craft Beer Renaissance. This final chapter serves as a reflection on the remarkable evolution of craft beer, from its humble beginnings to the vibrant and dynamic culture it is today. We celebrate the craft beer movement and the profound impact it has had on brewing, beer culture, and the community that surrounds it.

The Craft Beer Revolution Revisited

To understand the significance of the Craft Beer Renaissance, we must revisit the roots of the craft beer revolution.

Pioneers of Craft Brewing

We pay homage to the trailblazers who kickstarted the craft beer movement and set it on its path to success.

Defining Characteristics of Craft Beer

We reaffirm the defining characteristics of craft beer: small, independent, and innovative.

The Craft Beer Renaissance: A Global Phenomenon

The Craft Beer Renaissance has transcended borders, becoming a global phenomenon with a rich tapestry of local flavors and traditions.

Craft Beer's Global Reach

We explore how craft beer has spread worldwide, influencing brewing practices and cultures in diverse regions.

Local Terroir and Flavor

Craft brewers often draw inspiration from their local terroir, leading to the creation of unique and regionally distinct brews.

Brewing Innovation and Creative Expression

Innovation and creativity have been driving forces behind the Craft Beer Renaissance.

Boundary-Pushing Brews

We celebrate the audacious and experimental spirit of craft brewers who constantly push the boundaries of what beer can be.

The Intersection of Art and Science

Craft brewing is a harmonious blend of art and science, with brewers as both artists and engineers.

The Craft Beer Community: A Worldwide Family

The craft beer community is a global family, bound together by a shared passion for great beer.

Cross-Cultural Connections

We discuss the connections formed among craft beer enthusiasts from different cultures, languages, and backgrounds.

Solidarity and Support

The craft beer community demonstrates solidarity and support, especially during challenging times like the COVID-19 pandemic.

Beer Culture and Beyond

The influence of craft beer extends far beyond the brewing industry, shaping broader beer culture and consumption.

Craft Beer's Impact on Mainstream Beer

We explore how craft beer's focus on quality and flavor has influenced larger beer producers.

The Revival of Beer Tourism

Craft breweries have revitalized beer tourism, attracting visitors to regions known for their beer heritage.

Sustainability and Social Responsibility

The Craft Beer Renaissance champions sustainability and social responsibility, reflecting the values of its community.

Eco-Friendly Brewing Practices

We delve into how craft breweries prioritize sustainability, from energy-efficient equipment to waste reduction.

Community Engagement and Giving Back

Craft breweries often support local causes and communities through charity events and initiatives.

The Ongoing Evolution of Craft Beer

The Craft Beer Renaissance is an ever-evolving journey, with new chapters waiting to be written.

Emerging Beer Styles

We discuss emerging beer styles and trends that are shaping the future of craft beer.

Craft Beer's Influence on the Beverage Industry

Craft beer's innovative approach has influenced other beverage sectors, such as craft cider, spirits, and non-alcoholic alternatives.

Raising a Glass to Craft Beer

In conclusion, we raise a glass to the Craft Beer Renaissance and the remarkable community that has made it possible.

Celebrating Diversity and Inclusivity

We applaud the craft beer culture's commitment to diversity, equity, and inclusion, striving to make beer welcoming for all.

A Toast to the Future

As we celebrate the present, we look to the future, excited by the endless possibilities and innovations that await the world of craft beer.

Acknowledgments

We extend our heartfelt thanks to the brewers, beer enthusiasts, and communities around the world who have shared their stories, passion, and expertise to make this book possible. Craft beer is not just a beverage; it's a shared journey and a testament to the power of community and collaboration.

Prost to Craft Beer!

In the spirit of craft beer, we say "Prost!" to the Craft Beer Renaissance and the bright future that lies ahead for this beloved beverage. May the enthusiasm, innovation, and camaraderie that define craft beer continue to thrive and inspire generations of beer lovers to come. Cheers!

The Ongoing Evolution of the Craft Beer Movement

As we bring our exploration of the craft beer world to a close, we find ourselves at a juncture where the craft beer movement stands as a testament to the enduring power of innovation, community, and the love of beer. In this concluding chapter, we delve into the ongoing evolution of the craft beer movement, acknowledging the challenges it faces while celebrating the resilience, creativity, and potential that continue to drive its growth.

A Movement in Flux: Embracing Change

The craft beer movement has never been static; it thrives on change, adaptation, and forward thinking.

Responding to Consumer Preferences

We discuss how craft breweries are attuned to shifting consumer preferences, leading to the creation of new styles and flavors.

The Role of Technology

Advancements in brewing technology, from automation to quality control, are shaping the industry's future.

Innovations in Brewing Techniques

Innovation is at the heart of craft beer, with brewers continually pushing boundaries and experimenting with new methods.

Brewing with Unconventional Ingredients

We explore how brewers are incorporating unusual and local ingredients into their recipes, expanding the possibilities of flavor.

The Influence of Barrel Aging

The art of barrel aging has evolved, with innovative techniques and wood types influencing beer profiles.

The Rise of Collaborative Brewing

Collaborative brewing has become a hallmark of the craft beer movement, fostering creativity and camaraderie.

Global Collaboration Projects

We highlight international collaborations between breweries, transcending borders and cultures.

Brewer Exchange Programs

Some breweries engage in exchange programs, sending their brewers to work with other breweries to gain new insights.

Sustainability as a Driving Force

Sustainability is increasingly vital in brewing, with breweries embracing eco-friendly practices.

Reducing Environmental Impact

We explore how breweries are reducing waste, conserving resources, and minimizing their carbon footprint.

Supporting Local Agriculture

Craft breweries are often committed to sourcing ingredients locally, supporting regional agriculture.

The Revival of Historical Beer Styles

Craft brewers are resurrecting and reimagining historical beer styles, paying homage to the past while infusing creativity.

Rediscovering Forgotten Ales

We delve into the revival of ancient and historical beer recipes, offering a taste of bygone eras.

Traditional Brewing Techniques

Breweries are reviving traditional techniques such as open fermentation and decoction mashing for unique results.

Challenges and Resilience

While the craft beer movement has enjoyed immense success, it faces challenges that test its resilience.

Market Saturation and Competition

We discuss the impact of market saturation and the fierce competition among craft breweries.

Navigating Regulatory Hurdles

Craft breweries grapple with complex regulations and distribution challenges, often requiring innovative solutions.

A Global Craft Beer Community

The craft beer movement transcends borders, with a global community that fosters collaboration and exchange.

Cross-Cultural Inspiration

We highlight instances where brewers from different countries inspire each other, leading to cross-cultural brews.

The Craft Beer Diaspora

The craft beer movement has led to a global diaspora of brewers, sharing their passion and knowledge worldwide.

Beer Beyond Boundaries

Craft beer's influence extends beyond its own industry, shaping broader beer culture and consumption.

Influencing Mainstream Beer

Craft beer's impact on larger beer producers has led to improvements in quality and diversity.

The Craft Beverage Renaissance

Craft beer has inspired similar movements in cider, spirits, and non-alcoholic beverages, driving innovation across the beverage sector.

The Future of Craft Beer

The future of craft beer is filled with promise, with the movement poised to continue its evolution.

Exploring New Frontiers

We discuss emerging trends, from sour and wild ales to innovative beer formats like hard seltzers.

A Commitment to Inclusivity

We emphasize the importance of maintaining an inclusive and welcoming craft beer community for all.

Conclusion: A Never-Ending Journey

In conclusion, the craft beer movement is not just about beer; it's about the enduring spirit of exploration, creativity, and community. As it forges ahead into uncharted territories, the movement remains guided by its core values of quality, independence, and innovation. Craft beer continues to capture the hearts and palates of beer lovers worldwide, offering an ever-expanding tapestry of flavors, stories, and connections. As we raise a glass to the ongoing evolution of the craft beer movement, we look forward to the exciting chapters yet to be written in its story. Cheers to craft beer's boundless future!

Craft Beer's Influence on Beer Culture

The craft beer movement has not only transformed the beer industry but has also left an indelible mark on beer culture at large. In this concluding chapter, we delve into the profound influence that craft beer has had on the way we perceive, appreciate, and consume beer. From changing consumer preferences to inspiring new brewing traditions, craft beer's impact on beer culture is both significant and enduring.

Redefining Beer's Image

Craft beer has redefined beer's image, elevating it from a simple thirst quencher to a complex and artisanal beverage.

From Mass Production to Craftsmanship

We discuss how craft beer has shifted the focus from mass production to the artistry of brewing.

A Renaissance of Flavor

Craft beer has encouraged consumers to explore a wider spectrum of flavors and styles, challenging preconceived notions about beer.

The Shift in Consumer Preferences

Craft beer has played a pivotal role in shaping consumer preferences, fostering a demand for quality and diversity.

Embracing Local and Independent

We explore how consumers increasingly value local and independent breweries, seeking out unique and authentic experiences.

A Desire for Authenticity

Craft beer's emphasis on transparency and authenticity has influenced consumers' choices, favoring breweries with a genuine commitment to quality.

The Resurgence of Beer Education

Craft beer has sparked a renewed interest in beer education, inspiring enthusiasts to become more knowledgeable consumers.

Certified Beer Programs

We discuss the rise of certified beer programs like the Cicerone Certification Program, which offer structured education for beer enthusiasts.

Beer Appreciation and Tasting

Craft beer has encouraged beer appreciation and tasting as enthusiasts learn to discern and appreciate the nuances of different styles.

Exploring New Beer Styles

Craft brewers have been at the forefront of creating innovative and diverse beer styles, broadening the beer landscape.

The Proliferation of Styles

We delve into the diversity of beer styles that have emerged thanks to craft beer's experimental spirit.

Rediscovering Forgotten Styles

Craft breweries have resurrected forgotten or rare beer styles, preserving beer heritage and traditions.

Supporting Local Economies

The craft beer movement has bolstered local economies, driving tourism and supporting small businesses.

Beer Tourism and Destination Breweries

Craft breweries have become destinations, attracting tourists and boosting the economies of their regions.

Supporting the Supply Chain

Craft breweries often source ingredients locally, benefiting farmers and suppliers in their communities.

The Craft Beer Renaissance in Advertising

Craft beer advertising has challenged traditional beer marketing, embracing authenticity and storytelling.

Artistic Labels and Packaging

We explore how craft beer's creative labels and packaging have set it apart in the marketplace.

Telling the Brewer's Story

Craft breweries emphasize the brewer's story, connecting consumers with the people and passion behind the beer.

Nurturing a Spirit of Innovation

Craft beer's commitment to innovation has extended beyond brewing, inspiring change in the broader beverage industry.

Influence on Craft Spirits

We discuss how craft beer has influenced the craft spirits movement, with cross-pollination of ideas and techniques.

Expanding Craft Cider and Non-Alcoholic Beverages

Craft beer's impact has extended to other beverage categories, spurring innovation in cider and non-alcoholic drinks.

Fostering Inclusivity and Community

Craft beer has championed inclusivity, striving to make beer culture more diverse, welcoming, and equitable.

Diversity and Representation

We explore efforts to increase diversity and representation within the craft beer community, promoting inclusivity.

Community Engagement and Charity

Many craft breweries are actively involved in community initiatives, supporting local causes and fostering community bonds.

Craft Beer's Role in the Future

In conclusion, craft beer's influence on beer culture has been transformative, and its role in the future remains pivotal.

A Dynamic and Evolving Movement

We emphasize the dynamic nature of the craft beer movement, which continues to evolve and innovate.

A Legacy of Quality and Diversity

Craft beer's legacy is one of quality, diversity, and a deep appreciation for the craft of brewing.

Raising a Glass to Craft Beer

As we raise a glass to toast the craft beer movement and its enduring influence on beer culture, we acknowledge the dedicated brewers, passionate enthusiasts, and vibrant community that have made it all possible. Craft beer is more than just a beverage; it's a cultural phenomenon, a celebration of craftsmanship, and a testament to the power of innovation and community. In this ever-evolving world of beer, craft beer remains a guiding light, illuminating the path for the future of brewing and beer culture. Cheers to craft beer and all the flavors, stories, and connections it continues to bring to our lives!

THE END

Wordbook

Welcome to the glossary section of this book. Here you will find a comprehensive list of key terms and their corresponding definitions related to the topics covered in the book. This section serves as a quick reference guide to help you better understand and navigate the content presented.

1. Craft Beer: Beer produced by small, independent breweries that emphasize quality, flavor, and traditional brewing methods.

2. Microbrewery: A small brewery that produces limited quantities of beer, often with a focus on unique and innovative styles.

3. Macrobrewery: A large-scale brewery that produces beer in significant quantities and is typically associated with mass-produced, mainstream beer brands.

4. Craft Beer Movement: The collective effort by small, independent breweries to challenge the dominance of large, corporate brewers and promote artisanal, high-quality beer.

5. Brewpub: A combination of a brewery and a pub or restaurant where beer is brewed on-site and served alongside food.

6. Independent Brewery: A brewery that is not controlled or significantly influenced by a large beer corporation, maintaining its autonomy and craft focus.

7. Beer Styles: Distinct categories of beer characterized by their ingredients, brewing techniques, and flavor profiles, such as ales, lagers, stouts, and IPAs.

8. Hybrid Styles: Beer styles that combine elements from multiple traditional styles, resulting in unique and innovative flavor profiles.

9. Craft Brewers Association: A trade organization representing small and independent American craft brewers, promoting and protecting their interests.

10. Independent Seal: A symbol indicating that a brewery is independently owned and meets the criteria set by the Brewers Association.

11. Beer Boom: A period of rapid growth in the craft beer industry, marked by increased consumer interest and brewery openings.

12. Beer Culture: The collective customs, traditions, and practices associated with the production, consumption, and appreciation of beer.

13. Brewing Techniques: The methods and processes used in brewing beer, including mashing, fermentation, and conditioning.

14. Terroir: The unique environmental factors, such as soil, climate, and geography, that influence the flavors and characteristics of beer ingredients like hops and grains.

15. Beer Enthusiasts: Individuals who have a deep passion for beer, often seeking out new and rare brews, and engaging in beer-related activities and events.

16. Beer Festivals: Events where breweries showcase their products, allowing attendees to sample a wide variety of beers in a communal setting.

17. Online Communities: Virtual spaces, websites, forums, and social media groups where beer enthusiasts share information, reviews, and discussions about beer.

18. Beer Connoisseurs: Individuals with an advanced knowledge and appreciation of beer, often trained in beer tasting and evaluation.

19. Beer Trade: The exchange of beers between individuals, often involving rare or limited-edition brews.

20. Beer Tourism: Traveling to visit breweries, beer-related events, and regions known for their beer culture.

Supplementary Materials

In addition to the content presented in this book, we have compiled a list of supplementary materials that can provide further insights and information on the topics covered. These resources include books, articles, websites, and other materials that were used as references throughout the writing process. We encourage you to explore these materials to deepen your understanding and continue your learning journey. Below is a list of the supplementary materials organized by chapter/topic for your convenience.

Introduction:

Alworth, J. (2012). The Beer Bible. Workman Publishing Company.

Chapter 1: The Birth of Microbreweries:

Bamforth, C. W. (2009). Beer: Tap into the Art and Science of Brewing. Oxford University Press.

Mosher, R. (2009). Tasting Beer: An Insider's Guide to the World's Greatest Drink. Storey Publishing.

Chapter 2: Exploring Craft Beer Styles:

Jackson, M. (2010). Michael Jackson's Beer Companion: The World's Great Beer Styles, Gastronomy, and Traditions. Running Press.

Chapter 3: The Brewpub Revolution:

Oliver, G. (2012). The Brewmaster's Table: Discovering the Pleasures of Real Beer with Real Food. Ecco.

Chapter 4: Independent Craft Brewers and the Fight for Authenticity:

Acitelli, T. (2013). The Audacity of Hops: The History of America's Craft Beer Revolution. Chicago Review Press.

Chapter 5: The Craft Beer Boom and Its Impact on the Beer Industry:

Ogle, M. (2006). Ambitious Brew: The Story of American Beer. Houghton Mifflin Harcourt.

Chapter 6: The Art and Science of Craft Brewing:

Palmer, J. (2017). How to Brew: Everything You Need to Know to Brew Great Beer Every Time. Brewers Publications.

Chapter 7: Craft Beer Culture and Community:

Oliver, G. (2017). The Oxford Companion to Beer. Oxford University Press.

Conclusion:

Daniels, R. J. (2003). Designing Great Beers: The Ultimate Guide to Brewing Classic Beer Styles. Brewers Publications.

Papazian, C. (2003). The Complete Joy of Homebrewing. William Morrow.

www.ingramcontent.com/pod-product-compliance
Lightning Source LLC
LaVergne TN
LVHW012109070526
838202LV00056B/5673